Daughters and Lovers

Wesleyan University Press
Middletown, Connecticut

Daughters and Lovers

The Life and Writing of Mary Webb

Michèle Aina Barale

For Lynn

O sorella mia, "ciascuna è cittadina
d'una vera città; ma tu vuo' dire
che vivesse in Italia peregrina"

Copyright © 1986 by Michèle Aina Barale

.All rights reserved.

Frontispiece photograph of Mary Webb
by E. O. Hoppe, courtesy of the
Mansell Collection Limited, London.

Library of Congress Cataloging-in-Publication Data

Barale, Michèle Aina.
Daughters and lovers.

Bibliography: p.
Includes index.
1. Webb, Mary Gladys Meredith, 1881–1927.
2. Novelists, English—19th century—Biography.
3. Women in literature. I. Title.
PR6045.E2Z58   1986   823'.912 [B]   86-1298
ISBN 0-8195-5140-6 (alk. paper)

All inquiries and permissions requests should be addressed to the Publisher, Wesleyan University Press, 110 Mt. Vernon Street, Middletown, Connecticut 06457.

Distributed by Harper & Row Publishers,
Keystone Industrial Park, Scranton, Pennsylvania 18512.

Manufactured in the United States of America

First Edition

Contents

152935

Acknowledgments

Writing a book is a humbling experience; one feels isolated even as one realizes the absolute interconnectedness of scholarship. Not only are ideas and articles and books passed from hand to hand and mind to mind, but work is shared and even alleviated by the knowledge of others: Judi Knapp, who could make a cranky program produce a spotless manuscript; Anna Vayr, who always found ways to level what seemed the insurmountable; Michael J. Preston, who through many years has provided me with an office, desk, phone, typewriter, coffee, wine, and Scotch, as well as massive encouragement; Julie Willis, whose sharp mind and accurate eye offered me innumerable occasions of calm help and wry humor; Ursula Peters, who performed the onerous and therapeutic; Kathi George, whose practical knowledge and enthusiastic, patient, even long-suffering advice cannot be measured; R L Widmann, who proffered dinners, cheer, scholastic sensibility, and pragmatism. Gratitude is also due to the Lesbian Caucus/Feminist Alliance of the University of Colorado, Boulder, which provided me with a grant for materials and research, and to my Chair and colleagues in the Women Studies Program at the University of Colorado, who remained inexplicably patient with me throughout a most frantic year, and to the members of my dissertation committee, Richard J. Schoeck, James Kincaid, Mary Elizabeth Nelson, and Lee Chambers–Schiller, who worked with this manuscript in its most primitive state. In addition, I want to acknowledge the Woodrow Wilson Foundation for a grant when this manuscript was in its earliest stages, the University of Colorado for funding hard-to-find texts, and Jean D. Pfleiderer, who, generously and unasked, paid for the original typing of this manuscript.

Finally, I want to acknowledge all those who came before this book was thought of—mentors, writers, researchers, feminists and those who tried to be—who gave me what I needed, even when I didn't know that I did. And I want to thank all those who come after—my students, whose intellectual questioning and energetic discourse have so often stimulated my own thinking.

Daughters and Lovers

Introduction
Daughters and Lovers

Woman's efforts to achieve independence and an enlarge-
ment of her field of interests and activities are continually
met with a skepticism which insists that such efforts should
be made only in the face of economic necessity, and that
they run counter to her inherent character and her natural
tendencies. Accordingly, all efforts of this sort are said to
be without any vital significance for woman, whose every
thought, in point of fact, should center exclusively upon
the male or upon motherhood, in much the same manner
expressed in Marlene Dietrich's famous song, "I know only
love, and nothing else."

KAREN HORNEY, *The Overvaluation of Love*

Born in Shropshire, England, in 1881, and best known as
an author of rural romances, Mary Webb has been read all
too frequently as yet another woman writer of women's love
stories. Because her novels conclude, with one exception, in
the union of a happy couple who have achieved love despite
familial and social impediments to their happiness, audience
and critics alike have continued to value Webb for her romantic sensibilities. Although she has been valued as a realistic
depicter of British rural lives and, in this, often compared to
Thomas Hardy, her continuing appeal has been her emphasis
on love as the greatest human achievement and an unblushing
acknowledgment of sexuality's role in human lives. In her
focus upon love and sexuality, Webb is as legitimately compared to D.H. Lawrence as, in her focus on pastoral life, she
is to Hardy. Lawrence's belief in "a higher mystery," to be
best known and shared through sexual passion; his belief in
sexuality's power to enable human entrance into the larger,

I

and always mysterious, universe, echo Webb's own convictions. Both authors invest sexuality with mystical power and both view the sexual union of man and woman and the union of the human with the natural world as the catalysts of transcendence. Webb, *unlike* Lawrence, is indifferent to the social changes wrought upon country lives by industrialization, and disinterested in the changing mores of her age, but Webb, *like* Lawrence, offers the enactment of romantic love as the essential human drama.

Lady Chatterley's Lover differs from Webb's own romantic tales only in its sexual diction and social analysis. The romantic emphases of their stories are alike. So are the gender roles of lovers. Passive or wrongfully willful females give way to the passionate importunings of a male. Through that acquiescence the woman learns her true happiness and the man fulfills his natural power. Although Lawrence's male heroes are associated with a virile paganism and Webb's are Christ-like, both authors view male sexual power as mysticism's agent, and as providing the emotional intensity necessary to transcend the narrow confines of social institutions. Both authors place immense importance upon the necessity of romantic love's destruction of the rigid strictures of institutional morality if such love is to enable the lovers to transform themselves into unfettered, "natural" human animals. Webb, like Lawrence, acknowledges female sexuality, and for both, fulfillment of female sexuality is a consequence of male sexuality. Oliver Mellors teaches Connie Chatterley her name, her value, and her identity by teaching her his language: "Cunt! Eh, that's the beauty o' thee, lass"; Connie's meaning lies in Mellors' pleasure.[1] Although Lawrence's diction is hardly Webb's, she too depicts female identity as a male creation. Her heroines' most womanly act is submission to her lover.

It is, of course, this equation of female value with a male evaluator that characterizes Webb, in this sense, as a distinctly non-feminist author. She does write stories of female growth; she creates female characters who rebel against the restrictions of Victorian morality, characters who prefer the wider freedom of forest to the confines of parlor, who are sexually curious, and who possess the physical strength of men. Yet she forces her female characters ultimately to sacrifice autonomy and adventure in favor of love and marriage. She creates female characters who long for fame and fortune yet forgo these desires, a sacrifice that symbolizes their growth as good women. In female self-sacrifice resides female self-worth.

★   ★   ★

The justification of female selflessness in the cause of love seems greatly at odds with Webb's own life. Her rigidly pious and highly proper mother, Alice Meredith, had certainly fulfilled the roles assigned a woman of her class and time, yet she did not present to her daughter an image of the happiness to be gained through self-sacrifice. And her father, gentle and somewhat whimsical, hardly seems the virile dominator of his rather imposing wife. While the importance of Webb's marriage is indicated by her immense despair at its waning and by her struggle, even when mortally ill, to maintain it, Webb's writing and her need for an audience and for recognition were at least equally important as her marriage. It is not her life but her desire that generated her fiction. In her novels, unlike her life, women could choose love and marriage and be utterly content, totally fulfilled, needing nothing more.

It is this disparity between what Webb wrote and how she herself chose happiness that offers rich material for feminist analysis. That there is a distinction between art and life, even between art and author's life, is not in itself inexplicable. Such discrepancy, suggests Edward Said, is the very source of imaginative creation: novelistic fiction reflects desire and not fact, and the real world's harsh entrance into imagination's world serves to change the shape of authorial desire and thereby engender new imaginative visions, new fictions.[2] But what is the feminist reader and critic to make of a disparity between an author and her work when that disparity consists in the evaluation of a character as good, mature, and happy only when she denies the very things the author herself seemed most to value? How are feminists to read and judge novels in which a woman writer espouses as "right" the very life she herself would not and did not live?

This discrepancy is of interest to the feminist reader because it reflects a conflict of desires that is unique to women. Helene Moglen describes this as a struggle between "willed feeling and felt truth."[3] Woman's most deeply known truth is that she desires to create the self through the broadest possible experience of the world; she, like the male, would attain an independent, striving, acting identity. Such human desire is circumscribed by a myriad of constraints upon the process of female growth—constraints as overt as codes for female dress and behavior and as covert as the value-laden concepts of chastity, wifehood, maternity. Her desire for selfhood is in total opposition to what she must feel if she is to be "in love." Romance demands that she will herself to be dependent, passive, acquiescent to another, defined by her role as beloved— and therefore valuable—by another. She is no longer to strive to become herself; she is to strive to become someone else's. The desire to become an independent self in the world must give way to the need to become the dependent lover. Webb's novels reflect over and over again the conflict in a young woman who must choose between autonomy and romance.

The source of such conflict begins in the daughter's childhood education. As a daughter, Webb, like all daughters, learned from infancy such "willed feeling." It is the mother who is expected to foster society's values in her daughter; it is the mother, or her surrogate, who is the traditional teacher of womanhood. The mother's role as female educator is her second greatest source of value within the family; her greatest value, of course, is her reproductive ability. But neither her procreative role nor her role as educator is valuable in itself. Their true value lies in what they provide for their society: daughters who will emulate their mothers by falling in love, marrying, and producing sons to inherit the patrimony and daughters to learn their maternity so as to enable the continuance of another father's patrimony. Thus the daughter's most essential lesson in selfhood consists in her knowledge of her role as the biological and educational link in the chain of patrimonial inheritance. Such a lesson is the first in the daughter's education in romance.

If the mother's lessons teach domestication, the father's, at least in Webb's case, teach culture. Through her father's library and his literal schooling of her, Webb learned the broader worlds of literature and art. His many walks with her taught her nature and its observation. From his many conversations with her, she learned, we can presume, the wider world of male concerns and interests. It is her mother who teaches the daughter submission and her father who educates her in the world. *His* lesson appears by far more satisfying. Yet it is exactly all he has shown her, all he has trained her curiosity to consider, that she is expected to abjure in the name of romance, in the name of wifehood and maternity.

The irony of this education in romance is not lost upon Webb. All of her novels variously depict the educations provided to daughters by their parents. Her novels make it clear that the daughter's education in romance is her most important lesson. But they also repeatedly depict her parental teachers and their training as nonetheless flawed. It is only when a daughter learns her lessons outside the home that her education becomes a source of power—of self-identity—for her. In *Seven for a Secret,* Gillian Lovekin teaches the mute servant Rwth to read and write. Through her new-found literacy emerges the story of Rwth's past and her real name, her real parents, her true identity. In *Precious Bane,* Prue Sarn is taught to read and write by the local magician. These lessons enable her to control her brother's power over her, to court her lover, and ultimately to write the true account of her life, thereby putting to rest gossip and rumors. These lessons in literacy teach the daughter herself and enable her, in turn, to teach that identity to others. Although Webb creates daughters who are either murdered or married—or both—by her novels' conclusions, she also creates daughters who learn the power of language to create the self and fulfill its needs. Webb's novels accurately portray the daughter's lessons in romance as taken from a text filled with ellipses; nowhere within that education will she learn to name herself or learn the nature of her desires. Only when she is taught the lesson of language rather than of romance does she learn to utter her own name and speak her own being.

Such a depiction of female growth is appropriate to Webb's craft, writing, and to her own life, but inappropriate to her central theme, the primacy of romantic self-sacrifice. Yet the stories women write, read—and live—are love stories, or so the myth goes. The woman writer's most common tale is that of romance. It is romance, whether heterosexual or lesbian, that is commonly assumed to be the core of woman's existence. We have not yet found the means by which the ideology of romance can be happily integrated with our deepest sense of self.

In all of her novels, Webb struggled to find a definition of female happiness. She is adamant that such happiness lies outside her society's standards for female behavior. True identity, and, therefore, happiness, emerge only when an individual separates herself from the crowd and its mindless cant. The pleasures of sexuality and maternity have little to do with the institutions of marriage and motherhood, just as the profound joys of spirituality are not to be found in organized religion. Thus, for Webb, the real individual, the wholly formed woman, will always be at odds with society; happiness will be found only at the margins of culture.

Webb is entirely aware that her definition of happiness requires isolation. Often she attempts in her novels to find some means by which the gap between the isolated self and society can be bridged. It is love that connects individuals to one another and to the social whole. Two self-isolated individuals meet, fall in love, and, ultimately, marry. In that marriage they enter into an institution and thereby into society. But still, each acknowledges, the act is essentially superfluous. They know that they need no social approval or legal and moral codification of their love, yet they freely choose it. Thus the romantic embraces of Webb's conclusions are enacted by individuals who repudiate society's claims and dictates even as they perform the prescribed ritual of marriage proposal and ceremony. The contradiction is necessary for Webb to meet her fear of the consequences of complete alienation of the individual from her society.

However, in two of her novels, *Gone to Earth* and *Precious Bane,* Webb allows the individual's alienation to play itself out to, in one case, a tragic end and, in the other, a creative result. Hazel Woodus of *Gone to Earth* never does choose hearth over forest. Society's expectations for her behavior as a married woman do not offer her reason enough to renounce her woodland wanderings and settle down to making preserves. It is nature, however, not culture, that causes her death: too heavily pregnant, she cannot run to safety from a pursuing dog pack. *Precious Bane's* Prue Sarn would happily choose hearth and the comforts of a neighborly community if only she could. But, marked by her hare-lip, she is labeled a witch and a murderess. Yet Prue's affliction and consequent alienation result in both love and the pleasure and power of authorship.

A woman who showed neither interest in nor awareness of the issues surrounding "The Woman Question" of her own times, Webb offers the feminist reader a prime example of how the non-engaged woman writer was nonetheless intensely concerned with the nature of women's lives and happiness. Though Webb subverts the desires of her female characters, forcing them to abjure freedom for marriage, self for other, she depicts, sometimes, one suspects, in spite of herself, the struggle such abrogation of desire entails, and she portrays the forces, internal and external, that dictate women's choices. The frequent conventional conclusions of her novels are challenged by her inclusion of all the horrors of women's half-known lives: abortions, domestic brutality, rape, and even murder. She indicts mothers as well as fathers, church as well as family, society as well as the individual in her attempt to unravel the riddled nature of female happiness. What, where, or who, is the locus of blame for the dichotomy woman faces when she falls in love? Why is hers always the choice between self and other?

* * *

While woman's desire for love may take the socially ap-
proved forms of marriage and maternity or the less tolerated
shape of multiple brief relationships or even so-called "one
night stands," it is love, we are generally told, that woman
seeks and not sexual pleasure. Webb did not exclude the one
for the other. Although unlike women of her century, for
whom sexual desire even in marriage was considered suspect,
the contemporary woman is granted the right to erotic pleasure, and Webb had clearly insisted on that right in all of her
novels. But in her novels and in today's society woman is said
to enjoy sexuality and find principal satisfaction in the context of romantic love. Romance is the continuing context for
female sexual happiness.

Only a century ago the relationship between female anatomy and destiny was said to be fixed: the female body and,
most specifically, female reproductive ability not only determined but *assured* woman's future happiness if only she
heeded nature's demands. To fulfill her destiny was, therefore, to fulfill her body. For Webb, there was no escape from
such a destiny. In *Gone to Earth* Hazel Woodus's sole desire is
her right to live in the woods, free from social or moral constraints. She seeks to remain who and what she is rather than
be shaped by roles expected of her. But nature, Webb tells us,
demands growth and not stasis, and for women such growth
necessarily involves sexuality and, ultimately, children. Hazel
can either marry or she can die; she is no more free to escape
that dichotomized destiny than she is to escape her rapist or
deny her subsequent pregnancy. Woman's body, both its demands and its vulnerabilities, determines woman's happiness.

The relationship of female anatomy to destiny is no longer
fixed. The heart rather than the uterus is now said to be the
organ of women's destined joy. Despite the feminist movement, soap operas, pop psychology, novels, movies, songs,
and advertising reiterate that women must fall in love if they
are to be thought sexually fulfilled. Romantic love is based
on a culturally constructed ideology and rooted deep in
myth. Romantic and gothic novels fill the book stores; love

stories and soap operas dominate television and movie screens; lyrics about loving him, leaving him, finding him, losing him pervade popular music. Indeed, women's own conversations concentrate on romance as intensely if the beloved is female as if he is male. Women—heterosexual and lesbian—have "bought" the myth. Yet certain studies suggest to the contrary that women can and do enjoy sex without love and even that women are healthiest mentally and physically when they are single. Love is no longer woman's sure destiny.

Romantic love is an artifact of the dominant culture, of patriarchy; it is hardly surprising, therefore, that it fills the very air we breathe. Romance sustains patriarchy, which benefits from the sexual compliance of women who accept love's demands. But the model of power and dependency inherent in the ideology of romance does not explain its origins.[4] Love and marriage benefit patriarchy, yes. But patriarchy is as much *within* and dependent upon the ideology of love as are women. Men have also "bought" the myth. Men fall in love; like Chaucer's Troilus they grow pale and wan when love is unrequited, and anxious, angry, and frustrated when love is rejected. Not only do men believe that woman's desire for love is the predominant force operating in her life, a desire which forms her very identity as a human being, but they have believed in the importance of romantic love in their own lives, whether the object of love is male or female. For men, as well as for women, romance fulfills a profound psychic need.

Yet only women's identity is conceived of in terms of the emotion of love. Men fall in love and then "get on" with life; having acquired a mate and a mortgage, men move into the larger world and identify themselves in terms of other interests: profession, sport, hobby, clubs. Women fall in love and endlessly define and re-define themselves, their values and significance, in terms of that "fall," all their careers and worldly successes notwithstanding.

Novels of romance of necessity conclude with the romantic embrace and do not begin there. The story *after* the embrace is far less satisfying. There are the realities of debts and illness and age and death; and marriage, as Phyllis Chesler makes abundantly clear, all too often makes women mad—in both senses of the term.⁵ Madness, in literary romances, is the result of love left unrequited. But a realistic depiction of female domestic life would clarify all too well the facts that the romantic ideology idealizes: that the power imbalance perpetuated through gender roles results in one partner having wider boundaries and a larger sphere in which to create the self while the other partner's most important sphere of influence narrows to husband/lover, home, perhaps children.

There is a terrible irony in the fact that, while romance depends on gender roles, a narrowing of the realms in which the female self grows, the lovers are expected to experience mutual transcendence—loss of each self in that of the other—not loss of autonomy in the other's ascendancy. Each hopes to move beyond the boundaries of the physical and psychic self to achieve limitless union, a merging of identities. What is desired is itself genderless; what is achieved is a gendered power and importance. The institutions where love has primary power and value—marriage and the family—are gendered and therefore inherently unequal. Thus the very goal of romantic love cannot be attained because the structures in which it is to be achieved and enacted are built upon male dominance and female submission. It is not surprising that it is only a short leap from novels that end with the idealized romantic embrace of a passion-filled male and a swooning female (a conclusion Robert Rideout, the poet-lover of *Seven for a Secret,* endlessly writes and re-writes in his poems to Gillian Lovekin) to those novels in which the lover faints under the whip of the erotic dominator.

Both the novel of romance and the novel of sexual domination express a similar hope—entry into another, loss of identity's boundaries, *Liebestod*—either through orgasm or through sexual torture. Each partner expects the emotional satisfaction of union, but within a patriarchal structure, the bearer of the phallus—whether real or symbolic—is the dominator. When the woman holds the whip in romantic tales, we know that she will relinquish it. When she holds the whip in tales of sexual torture, we read the obverse story of a man who longs to experience the female swoon induced by the presence of a phallus. When two people have whips, we have a tale of competition. And if there are no whips? Then we have the story of friendship, but not of romance.

Mary Webb's novels, despite their emphasis on women's sexual curiosity and desire, hardly fit the category of literature usually defined as pornography. Yet they are, nonetheless, tales of female domination. While her female characters swoon at love and not at the whip, her insistence upon female submission and male power places her novels on the genteel end of a romantic continuum whose other end is the novel of physical domination. The rape of Hazel Woodus, Rwth's enslavement, torture, and murder are the darker, more clearly cruel depictions of the same romantic ideology that has Amber Darke of *The House in Dormer Forest* willingly acquiesce to her husband's demands that she sacrifice for him all that is most important to herself. Mary Webb agreed to the primacy of romance in women's lives—at least in her novels—but she remained utterly aware of the deadliness of such an agreement.

★　★　★

Webb's popularity, even two decades after her death, suggests how useful her readers found her novels. While it is certainly true that her audience in the early decades of this century found pleasurable escape from industrialization and war in her novels of rural lives and landscape, it is equally true that her female audience found in her romances the tales women have always sought in love literature. Webb's novels confirm female lives. Her novels delineated their readers' conflicts and justified their choice of romance and marriage. Women readers could find, in other words, reflection of their own known truth and depiction of their own willed feeling. The tale that enables the experience of her divided desire allows the woman reader to admit to her emotional consciousness all that remains still unresolved, but allows it entrance in the safe form of fiction: this is not me but another for whom

I feel such pain. The romantic embrace of Webb's conclusions confers further safety; despite the pain and anger the enforced decision between autonomy and love engenders, the choice of love is shown to be the proper one.

We come to the literature of love as much for instruction as pleasure, as much for assurance of our lives and choices as for escape from them. Daughters of our mother and our patriarchy, we have not yet discovered how we can also be lovers and ourselves. Webb does not offer the answer, but her sharp-eyed, irony-filled portrayal of the forces that shape the decision we make furthers Adrienne Rich's articulation of women's desire:

> I choose to love   this time   for once
> with all my intelligence.[6]

Author as Daughter

Awry in Eden

Women have had neither power nor wealth to hand on to
their daughters; they have been dependent on men as children are on women; and the most they can do is teach their
daughters the tricks of surviving in the patriarchy by pleas-
ing, and attaching themselves to, powerful or economically
viable men. . . .

ADRIENNE RICH, *"Jane Eyre: The Temptations of a Motherless Woman"*

Mary Webb was a child of her times. Like many other girls
in later Victorian and Edwardian England she was raised to
be a good woman in a world where even mediocre men had
more value, more power, and more freedom to pursue their
desire than any woman of talent. Most women were personally powerless in that public world. Yet their influence in
the domestic world was formidable. As mother, surrogate
mother, or governess, woman ruled the nursery and raised
the children long enough for her effect upon them to be deep
and lasting. Although the father's will prevailed, it was the
role of wife and mother to school their progeny. The son was
taught to expect to become father one day—a patriarch
whose will would be inculcated and enshrined in his own
children. But the daughter, like the mother who taught her,
would learn to teach the father's power to her own daughter;
hers was an education in subservience. This was the essential
maternal lesson to a daughter: her future power existed only
by ensuring his.

Carroll Smith-Rosenberg's study of nineteenth-century
American women's diaries suggests that the relationship between mothers and daughters was untroubled, tender, and

quite intense.[1] But such intimate and peaceful relationships were only possible when, as Margaret Homans points out, "these daughters had no other ambition than to become what their mothers were: good wives and mothers."[2] Identifying with their mother's role, most came to accept that role. A daughter who rejected the role of obedience had to create for herself a new role—a new way of being in the world. She had a double task—to create a new identity for herself, one not dependent on the social value that wifehood and maternity assured her, and to come to terms, make peace, with the maternal lessons from which she chose to stray. If, as Carol Dyhouse suggests, any mutual conflict and hostility between adolescent girls and their mothers lessened as the daughters themselves matured, married, and bore children, those daughters who did not reenact this female ritual may have continued to experience relationships of conflict and anger with their mothers.[3] The rebellious daughter, therefore, might find the chief obstacles to her personal autonomy not only the patriarch—possibly not even the patriarch—but her own mother. Although the mothers of some such girls took pleasure in their daughters' choice of autonomy over marriage, others reacted with envy, jealousy, or resentment. A daughter's rebellion could be interpreted as a rejection of the mother's values, and even a devaluation of the mother herself.

Elaine Showalter's description of Florence Nightingale's struggle with her mother for the time to study and work seems an apt description of the experience of daughters who chose literary over biological creativity: "The mother stood in the way of disciplined study, genuine self-improvement, and serious training" in a society in which "mother-daughter conflict was inevitable, in which each woman was enslaved to the other in a relationship of mutual incompatibility and incomprehension."[4] A poet-son could inherit the paternal mantle; a daughter who would write must reject the maternal apron. Yet, as Judith Pildes points out, "Even women who do not bear children are required to learn and practice maternal behaviour."[5] A daughter might reject the maternal model, but society would continue to view her—and judge her—in light of it. Such a daughter was Mary Webb.

★   ★   ★

Born March 25, 1881, in Leighton, Shropshire, to upper middle-class parents, Mary Gladys Meredith, to become Mary Webb, was the first of the six children of George and Sarah Alice Scott Meredith. Her early years, Gladys Mary Coles writes, were "an early experience of Eden, a personal paradise which enveloped her—literally in the Shropshire landscape. . . . And in this Garden of Eden her adored father was the central figure." Coles described Webb's relationship with nature and her father as one of "harmony, the sublime feeling of wholeness and changelessness. . . . For the rest of her life," Coles wrote, "she would strive to regain the inner vitality she experienced then. . . . She was never to cease in her striving to attain and retain wholeness. Whether obliquely or directly she would express the vision in all she wrote."[6] Webb's childhood is described as, in effect, Edenic by other Webb critics or biographers such as Barbara Hannah, Hilda Addison, Thomas Moult, and Dorothy Wrenn.[7] Her childhood is seen as a period of beneficent growth in the rural heart of nature, an image of pastoral country existence that softened the painful conflicts of life.

Webb's biographers, especially those of the 1930s, wrote to satisfy a craving for Webbiana that had as much to do with elegiac interest in rural lives as it did with Webb herself. The failure of two of her popular novels to win success on the stage in the 1930s—*Precious Bane* and *Seven for a Secret*—was, therefore, probably a consequence of their removal from this Edenic aura. The power and appeal of Webb's stories for this public depended on their natural setting. The landscapes of Webb's novels and of her life were as essential to them both as their own character.[8] A film version of *Gone to Earth,* made in the 1950s, was successful no doubt because it was shot on the Stiperstones and on Pontesford Hill. Critics described it as "a film in which Shropshire is the star." In W. Reid Chappell's *The Shropshire of Mary Webb* (1930) the reader could follow literally or imaginatively the woodland paths Webb had walked.[9] W. Byford-Jones's *Shropshire Haunts of Mary Webb* (1948) was a similar elegy to the simple and rural world.[10] Thus, Webb was enshrined as a "country mystic," a saint of rural lyricism, and her childhood and personal history were seen as consonant with her fiction and poetry. Both reflected the values a nostalgic public held most dear.

The impulse of Webb's biographers to give space and importance to her childhood geography is apt. Webb's descriptions of landscape are indeed the very matrix of her stories. Yet her life as seen within that rural setting deemphasized her life within her family and society. The real Mary Webb was far from a homely saint. She was sophisticated in her education, no untrained natural. She was complex, not simple, in her vision of nature; she saw nature as a meaning-filled system that pointed beyond itself. Eden had no daughters or sons; children were born to parents only after their eviction from the garden in shame and disgrace. Her Eden had snakes as well as apples. She drew from her childhood past a finely detailed memory of landscape, rural acquaintances, country cottages and estates, odors, sounds, colors, and shapes, but her Eden needed reshaping and re-creating if it were not to end as stories of Eden always do—with the woman's desire for knowledge entailing eternal loss of paradise for herself and her mate.

★   ★   ★

Mary Webb's mother, Sarah Alice Scott, was born May 6, 1852. Her father, a wealthy Edinburgh physician, died when she was a child. Her mother, Harriet Marian, was a formidable Victorian lady, who made sure that Sarah Alice was properly trained and educated. For a girl of her class and time, that education was primarily religious. Harriet Scott's will contained provision for such an education: her daughter was "to be educated by some Lady who will make religion the first consideration of her inheritance."[11] As an adult, Coles says, Alice Scott could quote at length from religious tracts; her manner was appropriately pious, although she lacked religious depth or feeling. Rigid, controlled, and precise, she preferred her flowers pruned and clipped rather than growing naturally in the Shropshire countryside. She married in 1880, at twenty-eight, when her husband, George Meredith, was nearly forty. Their first child, Mary, was born a year later.[12]

George Meredith was born in 1841. His father was headmaster of Newport Grammar School, and upon retirement became a vicar like his father before him. Rather than choose the church himself, as did his brother John, George Meredith earned an M.A. in classics from St. John's College, Cambridge. He was a teacher at the time of his marriage. In 1882, two years after their marriage, George and Sarah Alice Scott Meredith and their year-old infant daughter Mary moved to The Grange in Shropshire. It would be the family home for the next fourteen years. Five children were born there: Kenneth in 1888; Douglas in 1889; Muriel in 1890; Olive in 1891; and Mervyn in 1894. With their move to The Grange, George Meredith began to take in private pupils for coaching for entrance into the universities. He also became a gentleman farmer. Managed by a bailiff, the farm was a source of fresh produce for the large household of family, servants, and schoolboys, and a soothing occupation for George Meredith himself, "a kind of pastoral lullaby."[13] The Merediths were decidedly "country-house people," as Douglas Meredith said.[14] Farming was a pastime and pleasure but hardly a means of subsistence, as it was for cottage folk. The Merediths were a middle-class family; as in other middle-class families of the time, income was supplemented by inherited wealth. The rather considerable Scott estate later would provide an annual allowance for all the Meredith children.

Mary Webb had all the advantages that well-educated, moderately well-off, and somewhat liberal parents could give their eldest daughter. It would have been hard to become a woman writer under any circumstances, but nearly insurmountable if Mary Webb had grown up in an urban working-class or a rural cottage family. Flora Thompson writes that girls and women of the cottages were so burdened with endless tasks of housework, child care, and making ends meet

that they had neither time nor energy for education beyond
the rudimentary.[15] Although the picture of the middle-class
country-house daughters that Webb draws in *The House in
Dormer Forest* is darkly depressing—covertly powerful mothers endlessly attempt to stifle the spirits and lives of their
daughters and sons through the imposition of rigid Christian
formula and stultifying social ritual—she also writes of girls
who do receive an education and who have the leisure to read,
to write, and to dream. Because of her mother's rigid sense
of propriety, Mary Webb no doubt was trained in the domestic arts. But as an adult she did her best not to employ that
training; she hated housework and avoided it. She saw herself
as educated for other things.

Victorian schools for girls tended to reinforce home values
and to subordinate values of the intellect to femininity. Some
twenty years before Mary Webb's childhood, the Royal Com-
mission's investigation of the British educational system had
concluded that girls' schools demonstrated a "want of thor-
oughness and foundation; want of system; slovenliness and
showy superficiality; inattention to rudiments; undue time
given to accomplishments, and these not taught intelligently
or in any systematic manner."[16]

As Carol Dyhouse has shown, home education was de-
signed primarily "to school a girl in femininity." And academic goals were deemed of minor importance, for
women.[17] Still, "the academic value of a girl's home education," Dyhouse says, "would vary with the extent to which
her parents cherished intellectual, literary, or other cultural
values, and in connection with this, with the parents' choice
of a governess."[18] Many women who were to achieve successful academic careers had been well educated at home and
had prepared themselves through private study for the university.[19] The education Mary Webb received at home was
certainly better than she might have received at a local girls'
school or in the typical home. It was hardly rudimentary,
superficial, or without plan although it necessarily lacked the
urbanity and sophistication of Virginia Woolf's own London
education. So well trained was Mary Webb at home that

when her mother decided she should attend Mrs. Walmsley's finishing school in Southport, Lancashire, she was accused of cheating at French because her teachers were surprised by her facility. Most girls of the period learned far more about muffins and roasts, linens and needlework, than they did about French and mathematics. But Webb, who had a first-rate mind, was given the materials to expand and develop her intellect. In this respect, she does not appear to have been limited by her sex.

Her home education stressed reading, writing, and memorization. By the time she was an adolescent, she knew much of Shakespeare by heart; she had written and acted in home-made plays, and she had produced a handwritten volume of poems. She had been tutored in landscape painting by her father, who was a cousin of David Cox, a painter, and he entered his daughter in his own first-form classes when she was barely old enough. When she was eleven, a young woman, Miss Edith Lory, was hired to tutor her. Miss Lory became a life-long confidante and in her care Mary Webb would die. Miss Lory, called Minoni by the family after the tongue-tied attempts of the Meredith children at pronouncing her name, was warm and humane, much loved by the children.[20] Under her tutelage, Webb read the major poets and contemporary writers—Hardy, Jefferies, Housman, and Kipling. In her early twenties she read Bennett, Darwin, and Haeckel—books provided by her brothers,[21] the two oldest of whom had been sent in their early teens to Ellesmere College, a Shropshire boarding school of good reputation. She did not attend the university, yet her physical illness from the time she was nineteen until she was twenty-two would, in any case, have precluded that. But if she had been sent to the university, would she have been ill at all? When she recovered she did attend Cambridge Extension lectures, and was respected there for her acuity and critical perception.

Ellen Moers suggests that a history of literary feminism can be found in the metaphor of women walking.[22] The adolescent girl or the house-bound woman left the confines of home to discover in the larger world of garden or woods a locus of freedom. I suggest that such a history exists also in the metaphor of women reading. Books, like a garden or forest, could be an escape. A woman like Webb had access to both routes to a larger, freer world. She had access to nature and access to a private library. A woman with university-trained brothers, a woman with a schoolmaster for a father, she had entry into worlds beyond the Shropshire hills.

Webb's biographers consider her country walks and naturalist observations the source of her greatest childhood pleasure. That passionate love of nature is indeed apparent in all her writing. Her pleasure in nature was a refuge from the confines of home and her mother's critical eye. She went outdoors because she could not happily remain within.

For Mary Webb, books and nature were the means by which the self could be sought, created, and ultimately re-created in triumph. Language gave her the means to *create* herself as subject. Nature offers the female adolescent refuge and a landscape in which, suggests Simone de Beauvoir, she can *experience* herself as subject:

At home, mother, law, customs, routine hold sway and she [the female adolescent] would fain escape these aspects of her past; she would in her turn become a sovereign subject. But, as a member of society, she enters upon adult life only in becoming a woman; she pays for her liberation by an abdication. Whereas among plants and animals she is a human being; she is freed at once from her family and from the males—a subject, a free being. She finds in the secret places of the forest a reflection of the solitude of her soul and transcendence; she is herself this limitless territory, the summit flung up toward heaven; she can follow these roads that lead toward the unknown future, she will follow them; seated on the hilltop, she is mistress of the world's riches, spread out at her feet, offered for the taking.[23]

Books were also keys to an unknown future, to becoming a "sovereign subject," a true self. Among books, she too, could be "a human being."

What women read and what reading offered to them is a study of its own, already admirably begun with Elaine Showalter's *A Literature of Their Own*.[24] In *The Madwoman in the*

Attic, Sandra Gilbert and Susan Gubar describe *Wuthering Heights* as a female vision of paradise in which the satanic is made sacral.[25] Mary Webb had read and read well this novel in which the theme of women and books predominates: at the beginning young Cathy longs for her books, and at the end she teaches Hareton to read those books. Catherine Earnshaw's punishment for her transgressions against female propriety is the denial to her of the books she cherished and the enforced reading of damnation-threatening religious texts; it is between the pages of just such a text that Catherine keeps the journal that reflects her deviance from moral strictures. In a number of other nineteenth- and twentieth-century novels, including Webb's own, the relationship between girls, education, and books plays a significant role.

Between Mary Webb's sixth and twelfth birthdays, her mother gave birth to her other five children. Alice Meredith had domestic help, but she had the responsibility for planning meals and budgets, accounting for linens and time schedules, and ensuring that husband, children, pupils, and servants were adequately cared for and properly employed. In addition, she ran a boarding academy and carried out diverse social and religious duties. Webb's biographers describe Alice Meredith as cold and withdrawn, rigidly punctual, highly organized; yet these are qualities one might consider virtues in carrying out such multiple responsibilities. Still, she was not a happy woman and her personality, seen from the distance of nearly a century, appears so opposite to her husband's that a modern reader might suspect that their marriage endured simply because endurance was expected.

George Meredith seems to have been as warm, generous, and humorous as his wife was not. He was casual and informal, enjoying the rougher aspects of gardening in clothes more appropriate to his outdoor help than to the master of the house. His many pieces of light verse give evidence of a man who could enjoy the humorous side of his own character. It was Mary Webb's father who introduced her both to learning through his library and his teaching and also to the careful observation of nature and the vision of nature as a means of spiritual entrance into a transcendent mystical realm. With him she began her country walks. As was often the case, it was the father who provided the daughter with the vision of the larger worlds of books and nature, while the mother was left to impose the restrictive duties of domesticity. The matriarchal role as enforcer of discipline, which Alice Meredith assumed, enabled George Meredith to indulge in the unhindered pleasures of paternity. He was free to be indulgent and to gain his eldest daughter's unqualified love and admiration; the mother was relegated to ensuring that his wishes were fulfilled. In the domestic world in which men were indulged, the common stereotype of distant, severe, discipline-imposing patriarch was, in the Webb family, at least, more characteristic of the mother than the father.

The crucial first fourteen years of Webb's life seem to have been secure ones. She was financially well cared for, educationally cultivated, and emotionally provided for by her father and by her governess. When in 1895 she was sent to Mrs. Walmsley's in Southport, she was wrenched from her safe and interest-filled nest. She remained at the school for less than a year, because in 1895 her mother fell from her horse in a hunting accident and Mary was brought home to superintend the running of the house. She directed the several servants, organized the household, became surrogate mother to her younger brothers and sisters (Mervyn was ten months old), surrogate mistress of house and academy, and surrogate wife to her father. Her biographers say that she found great satisfaction in fulfilling these roles, although they directed her toward the narrower world of household care. Hardly more than a child herself, she alternately mothered and played with the children. She took upon herself the tutoring of the youngest girls, and cared for her father's material needs as much as possible, while directing the several members of the household staff with the understandable inefficiency of an adolescent. She put aside the world of intellect for the world of domesticity, but with it came the kind of autonomy and adult power that were bestowed on women in the private realm.

In her upstairs bedroom, Alice Meredith relinquished to

her daughter the power, along with the burden, of managing the domestic scene. But she retained the negative maternal power of criticism. When the children were paraded after breakfast and supper to greet their mother, often with small gifts, she criticized any offerings that seemed inadequate. She was now an even less loving and more remote figure than before. Her children regarded her with dutiful but not heart-felt respect, and Mary became the central figure in their lives.[26]

Mary Webb's new responsibilities brought her new independence. She was a free agent during her long days while the household staff went about their tasks. She might be called upstairs to be upbraided, but once downstairs she could indulge in a freedom unusual for a middle-class girl, one not possible at Mrs. Walmsley's. Her principal pleasures were her day-long expeditions into the countryside, where she would bicycle for miles to spend the entire afternoon lying in a field or picnicking in the woods. She would leave home after breakfast and return at dinnertime; her whereabouts were never questioned.[27] She could escape from the normal confines of middle-class existence that most girls her age had to endure. That escape into long days of laborless observation encouraged her detailed memory of nature, and decades after her death her audience would read her novels for their description of a fading rural England. The extraordinary immediacy of her depictions of country lives convinced her readers that the author had lived the lives of her characters, that she was intimate with cottage life, the sheepfold, the pasture.

For five years, until she was nineteen, Webb maintained her position as de facto mistress of the house. Then one morning in 1900 Alice Meredith appeared unannounced at the breakfast table, cured of her illness, critical of all she saw, and prepared to resume control of household, children, and husband. The exact nature of Alice Meredith's illness is not known. She had suffered a spinal injury in her fall, yet after a while the injury did not prevent her getting up and walking about her own room, nor did it interfere with her living a long life thereafter: she lived thirty years after the accident and did not suffer during her old age. Wrenn believes the illness was primarily hysterical, a byproduct of her desire to free herself from the burdens of further childbearing and the demands of nursery and kitchen and parlor, and the demands of her life in a small town she disliked. Coles suggests that her illness enabled her to achieve "psychological with-drawal." [28]

Wrenn speculates that Alice Meredith's Victorian sense of duty would not permit her to continue to ignore her family; Wrenn believes that she realized that her husband was totally impractical about the household budget, and that Mary was not only impractical but extravagant, ordering food and clothing as desired rather than as needed. And, with fewer pupils in the academy, the family finances were greatly strained—so much so, in fact, that in 1896 The Grange was sold and the family moved into a less expensive house, The Woodlands, some fifteen miles from Much Wenlock. [29]

When Alice Meredith returned to family life, her youngest child was six, old enough to be given over to the care of Miss Lory; nursery days were over. The two youngest girls were nine and ten, old enough not to demand their mother's constant attention, and the boys were away at school. Mary was certainly old enough to be mistress of her own household had she been married. But with her mother's return, she was no longer bound but no longer privileged. She was replaced, and her independence was curtailed. Her mother forbade the long rides in the country and allotted tasks for her to perform. The daughter who had been mother became daughter once again. She lost the self-rule in which she had taken such pleasure, and she ceased to be the focus of her adored father's attentions: "Worst of all to her was the realization that her adored father no longer needed her—never had needed her. For all the years of her mother's illness, she had basked in the happy certainty that it was she who had been the center of his life. All that she did had been for him, while Mamma, in her room upstairs, had been nothing but an uneasy shadow." [30]

It is not difficult to understand the daughter's sense of displacement; having been her father's caretaker, she had also been the focus of his interest. What is not so initially apparent in this aspect of Webb's early life—but what is nonetheless quite likely—is that the reversal of roles the daughter underwent would have, in a sense, sexualized her relationship with her father. This is not to suggest that there was even the vaguest sort of sexual activity between father and daughter, but rather that the role of mother is invested with sexuality and that she who takes on the maternal role takes on, as well, that role's sexuality. Daughters who marry and become mothers are legitimately invested with a sexual relationship, but when mothers become daughters once again they are divested of that sexuality. Alice Meredith's return to the parlor deprived her daughter of self-determination and her father's conversation and attention, and displaced the sexualized bond of intimacy and sharing between husband and daughter.

It is one thing to be relieved of the onerous duties of maternity and domesticity—of trading and tending, watching and mending; it is quite another to be replaced in the position of wife, because with that role comes the power and prestige that accrued to the wife of a gentleman-farmer. Although none of the biographers suggest that Alice Meredith had been jealous of her daughter's surrogate role and its resultant privileges, privileges that included evenings spent in long conversations with her father, and although there is no suggestion that Mary was angry with her mother for ending these pleasures, Alice Meredith did come downstairs just when her daughter was old enough to become real mistress of the house. Mary returned to her mother the role of mistress and in exchange took on her mother's role of invalid. For the next two years, listless, moody, painfully thin, Mary lay propped by cushions on the sofa in the drawing-room—her illness always visible to the family and the family's life always visible to her.[31]

This is too tempting a family portrait not to examine further. The invalid mother upstairs, then the invalid daughter

downstairs: illness—a woman's illness—seemingly always at
the heart of the family. One woman enters into illness with
the giving of birth and then as the only honorable means of
escape from babies and social burdens. The other finds in
illness a sure method of passive power. Ill, Mary, like her
mother before her, needed constant tending, becoming in a
sense the helpless child Alice Meredith thought she had defended herself against in evading further pregnancy but now
was faced with again. Prostrate, Mary Webb could not be
subject to her mother's demands and social plans, and was
hardly in a position to receive her mother's criticism of her
household management. It is difficult not to speculate on
Mary Webb's illness as a possible means of simply not
"seeing" her mother resume her rightful place with her father. If she no longer had independence and power, she might
as well be invalid. If it was now Alice who conversed at dinner with George Meredith, and Alice who sat next to him in
the evening, Mary at least was spared from having to take a
lesser seat at the table, a lesser place in the sitting-room, a
chair now apart from her father's side. Mary could neither
fight for her old position with her father nor for her old role
within the household; she had neither the strength nor the
right to do so. A son does not assume the father's burdens
and cannot assume the father's role until the father relinquishes it. A daughter, however, is expected to share her
mother's burdens, though not her role as wife; she can only
assume her power when that power is willingly given over.
Mary Webb's mother relinquished both for a time, then took
them back. With Alice Meredith's resumption of household
and wifehood, Mary quite literally found a position from
which she could not compete. Illness and its enforced passivity brought a certain safety and a returned measure of power.
This was a maternal lesson Webb learned thoroughly and
never forgot.

At first the doctor diagnosed anemia and prescribed fresh
air and exercise. But the exertion proved to have adverse effects and the patient became still more ill. A young woman's

ailments were often diagnosed as anemia during the turn of the century. It was the mark of a modern doctor to suggest that the best cure was activity and exercise—young women's bodies were no longer considered frail vessels in constant danger. The psychological aspects of wan listlessness were not ignored; a young woman might cease eating, sleep poorly, and lack strength because she brooded too much. But it was not anemia or depression that was the most likely cause of Webb's first illness or of the setback after the initial diagnosis. The cause was later diagnosed as Graves' disease, exophthalmic hyperthyroidism, at that time essentially incurable. The disease results in high fever, quickened metabolism, fluctuating emotions, intense nervousness, and severe gastric disturbances. In addition, it has visible effects: the enlarged thyroid gland at the base of the throat—a goiter—and the eyes thrust outward, protruding and staring, barely able to be covered by the lids—exophthalmia. It is an illness with severe emotional effects, and one in which emotional upset can cause a sudden worsening of symptoms. Both depression and anxiety are the results of the disease; they are also the cause of its recurrent flare-ups.[32]

This change from active and independent adolescence into a semi-invalidism marked the end of Webb's youth. But she was not a passive victim. During the three years of her illness she read extensively and began her writing career. What she read most certainly affected what she wrote. Although she never forgot the lesson of infirmity she had learned from her mother, she nurtured a strong desire to regain at least psychic health. Her writing, as an act of self-expression, was, by the very nature of authorship, an attempt to exert herself, her power, her own view of the world. It was a means of changing the world and shaping it to her own designs. It was, in other words, an activity of health, a demonstration of self-determination, and, at the same time, an activity she was free to carry out only because illness gave her the time and freedom to do so. Had Webb remained healthy after her mother's resumption of the household, her time certainly would have

been consumed by the multiple duties of marriage or the social duties unmarried daughters of her class were expected
to assume. Time to read and write would have been minimal.

Webb's recumbent posture mirrored neither psychic nor
creative paralysis. The young gentlemen of this period went
out into the world to make their way and seek their fortune,
but because that particular journey was not possible for
young women, the means for such self-seeking was to be
found in the restricted world of the couch—in a world the
width of a bed. Webb's illness was not a conscious creation;
nor was it for Elizabeth Barrett Browning, or Florence
Nightingale, or the many other women who took to their
beds. While their sense of enclosure, or even impotence, may
have been consciously acknowledged, it is difficult to believe
that the consequent act of self-immurement was willed. For
Alice Meredith, also, the sickbed had provided relief from
the endless duties of wifehood, maternity, social and church
life. It had enabled her to wield a covert power, as well. Elizabeth Barrett Browning and Florence Nightingale—and
Mary Webb—freed from domestic tasks, were prodigiously
productive while prostrate.

Webb's invalidism was a fact and factor in her life, with
both literal and symbolic significance, both social and personal metaphor. Her disease would ultimately contribute to
her death at the early age of forty-six, just as her literary fame
seemed certain. She would become an invalid again during
times in her life that were particularly unbearable. But such
is the nature of Graves' disease, and such is the nature of that
other disease which, although various in its manifestations,
was widely diagnosed as hysteria and which sent so many
women of her era and class to their beds for weeks and
months and years on end. It is a disease with an etiology as
much social and familial as physical—if, in fact, physical at
all. Smith-Rosenberg suggests that hysteria is a "socially recognized behavior pattern and as such exists within the larger
world of cultural values and role relationships."[33] It was not
only recognized but accepted, and in certain situations en-

couraged; female illness was proper female behavior. As long as individual domestic roles are rigidly defined, "hysteria can be seen as an alternative role option for particular women incapable of accepting their life situation."[34] In such situations, passivity becomes the better part of womanly valor, enabling a woman to carry out the behavior and good breeding her society deemed feminine. She *could* become what was socially accepted as a fitting woman; she needed only to be ill.

Psychoanalyst Juliet Mitchell discusses the relationship between hysteria and authorship in woman's writing.[35] It is too simplistic to claim that some women suffering from a socially induced dis-ease—hysteria—write novels that of necessity reflect their discomfort of mind and body. Mitchell understands hysteria as the very precondition of female authorship in a capitalistic society: "The woman novelist must be an hysteric. Hysteria is the woman's simultaneous acceptance and refusal of the organization of sexuality under patriarchal capitalism. It is simultaneously what a woman can do both to be feminine and to refuse femininity, within patriarchal discourse."[36] To write as a woman in such a society is to write as an hysteric since "the hysteric's voice" is *the woman's masculine language* (one has to speak 'masculinely' in a phallocentric world) talking about feminine experience."[37] There is, in other words, a disparity between the woman writer's self and experience and the phallocentric language available to her. Mitchell's concept of "hysteria" as woman's authorial tongue suggests that in the act of literary translation of female experience into male speech, there is a linguistic disturbance which mirrors her social condition as marginalized being, as Other. Hysteria, in Mitchell's context, thus becomes not the sign of authorial—that is to say, *female*—neurosis, but the accurate reflection of the woman writer's position in a patriarchal culture. Women must write in a foreign (male) tongue; when they so write, they sound "hysterical." For Mitchell, the phrase "hysterical woman writer" is utterly redundant.

Webb was never willing to give in totally to her illness until it finally prostrated her. But when she was suffering most

severely, during her late thirties and early forties, discoveries
had been made by American doctors that would have alleviated her symptoms, possibly even cured her. She was ad-
vised by Rebecca West, whose mother suffered from the same
illness, to seek such treatment as quickly as possible since it
was successful only when administered during the early
stages, but Webb refused.[38] Her stubborn will fought to overcome on her own everything that might impede the satisfaction of her desire to succeed, and she resented the implication
that she could not do so on her own, that she needed help of
any sort. But that refusal also reflects her need to cultivate a
psychic dimension that demanded that she be "marked"—
that she remain victim, the pain-wracked poet-observer, yet
equipped with a language of creativity that could transcend
pain and stigma. Even this early in her life, we see evidence
of Webb's conflicting desires for health and power, on the one
hand, and for passive suffering on the other.

In the first attack of Graves' disease Webb spent nearly two
years in bed and another year recovering further. Unlike her
mother in her illness, Webb allowed no one but family to see
her for months. Though she had always been shy, she now
became wholly introverted. When, after three years, she finally began to go outside again she was painfully aware of
her changed appearance. Disease had, indeed, left its actual
"mark" upon her. Alice Meredith reminded her daughter of
her physical defects by her display of displeasure. Townspeople, even years later, remembered the mother's negative
response to her pop-eyed and goitered daughter who was
emaciated and shy to the point of pain. Wrenn, interviewing
several Shrewsbury residents who had known the Meredith
family during the time Mary Webb was living at home,
quotes one in particular: "Her sisters . . . were bonnie girls
but Mary was very plain, poor thing. I never liked the
mother—she was a hard mother, and seemed very conscious
of Mary's ugliness, as if she resented her for it."[39]

Webb now began to suspect that she was being sold poisoned food by the town grocers, and she refused to buy stock
from the same shop twice in a row.[40] Although this fantasy

of poisoning did not persist for long, it reappeared briefly some years later, and signaled the beginning of her lifelong difficulty with food and eating. Webb would feed others, but often failed to feed herself. After her marriage, she would give away food she did not have the money to replace, subsisting on bread and tea. Afflicted with an illness that required a particularly rich, caloric diet, Webb, a vegetarian since early childhood, denied herself those few foods rich in the iron and protein that her vegetarianism allowed.

It is tempting to view Webb's lifelong difficulty with food—both her refusal to eat more than her meager bread and jam and her fear of poisoned food—as evidence of the "modern" eating disorder, anorexia. Some studies of women diagnosed as anorexic suggest that such women come from homes characterized by rigid strictures on female behavior, unemotional familial interaction, and dominating mothers who demand that their daughter's growth reflect maternal hopes and desires. This describes Webb's family, yet one hesitates to affix the label of anorexic. The supposition that anorexic women stringently control their eating because it is the one area of a chaotic world over which they can have power does *not* seem descriptive of Webb, nor does the anorexic's preoccupation with weight and fear of obesity. Webb does appear to have "trouble with food" as do so many contemporary women. But from this distance in time it is difficult to know the exact nature of her disorder.

★ ★ ★

To avoid public scrutiny, Webb went on long, solitary walks in the countryside of Meole Brace. The period 1902–3 was one of ambulatory convalescence during which she began to write the poetry and essays that fourteen years later would be published as *The Spring of Joy*. Her nature walks were essential to her physical and spiritual mending. In her first essay, "Vis Medicatrix Naturae" she writes:

The power of this life, if men will open their hearts to it, will heal them, will create them anew, physically and spiritually. Here is the gospel of the earth, ringing with hope, like May mornings with bird-song, fresh and healthy as fields of young grain.[41]

Although she is adhering to the conventions of her time in the use of male pronouns and collectives, Webb is clearly delineating her own experience in the natural world. Hers, too, are the soul's adventures in *The Joy of Motion:*

Those who have complete bodily freedom will probably never enter fully into the deep happiness brought by waving grass and running water; but he who has time and who cares to use his imagination, can see in all natural things the bowing down of the creature before the Creator. . . . A watcher of the melodic ritual of earth cannot know stagnation of soul; his ideas are fresh and vigorous. Although the healthy quickening of the pulse after exertion, the joy of hard work, may be denied to a man, adventures of the soul are his. . . . Who can say that such enterprises of an eager spirit may not be nearer to real life—the life of the unknown forces that hold the wandering star and guide the traveling moon—than are the more comprehensible adventures of the body?[42]

Earth's gospel, the superiority of the quiet watcher to the active person, the adventures of the soul versus those of the powerful body, the greater satisfaction found in spiritual comprehension contrasted to physical mastery of the natural world—these are the themes of her earliest work, the essays. They are consistent throughout all her work. That they are so constant indicates that they were far more than philosophical musings borrowed from Richard Jefferies or second-hand impulses taken from Wordsworth. Webb walked and healed, reflecting, in her physically mending body and in her writing, the processes of the natural rural world. She was aware of the enormous energy of the world of plant and animal: "In nature there is sure harbour: for things that once engrossed the mind begin to look pale and small when seen in conjunction with the immense, brilliant perspectives of hill and sky: so life's values right themselves again."[43] If she began to walk into the country because of morbid dread of the eyes of the townspeople, she continued because she became strong. Quite often in Webb's life, the psychically unhealthy undertaking leads to healthy action, but perhaps at no time so clearly as here. And no other woman writer has so articulately presented the act of nature walk as healing as has Webb in these

essays. Men walk and write of it in detail: the amateur naturalist amid the country lanes was not a rare posture for the
essayist during Webb's lifetime, nor even during our own.
The great Romantic writers toured with passionate vigor:
Wordsworth, Keats, Coleridge, Shelley, Nietzsche, Whit-
man, Goethe—all were writers who walked the rural landscape. Women walked as well: and they also observed. The
currently popular *Country Diary of an Edwardian Lady* indicates that the natural world was considered a fitting subject
for the amateur female artist.[44] But no other woman writer
describes as thoroughly as Webb her own healing through
nature observation or so deliberately writes literary essays—
not religious tracts, not medical literature—that are concerned with the diseased perceptions caused by physical illness. No other woman literary figure has produced a series
of essays concerned with healing the body of invalidism and
the soul of a morbid dread of death. Her reading and education, her sense of nature's interrelationship with psyche, her
need to immerse herself in the world of plants and animals,
trained her in that literary tradition. She begins her essays
with an epigraph from Sir Thomas Browne: "We live the life
of plants, the life of animals, the life of men, and at last the
life of spirits."[45]

Webb became ill in 1901, convalesced in 1902–3, and until
1911 carried out her role as the unmarried, infirm, physically
marred daughter who remained at home. Although the worst
symptoms of Graves' disease—the goiter and the exophthalmia—disappeared for some years, she remained unusu-
ally thin and frail. Still she was expected to fill her time
with constant—and trivial—obligations. Townspeople assured Wrenn that the Meredith family entered as fully into
the life of the town as their social standing demanded. George
Meredith, in his rambling walks every afternoon, stopped to
chat with the neighbors; Alice Meredith made friends with
the vicar and took upon herself far more church work than
she could fulfill. The overflow was delegated to the Meredith
daughters, and to Mary, the eldest, in particular.[46] For six
years, Mary made parish visits, which, considering her hor-

ror of being seen, must have been most difficult. Were it not for the essays, written during this time, we would know nothing of her inner life. They are examples of the hidden life lived by so many women, married and unmarried, during this era.

In 1909, after a year-long illness, George Meredith died. Webb was grief-stricken and again became ill, nursed by her grieving mother. In "Treasures," a poem written for her father, she notes the physical reminders of his now lost presence: flowers he loved, trees he planted, the echo of his laugh, and his hand placed lovingly on her hair, treasures that must be kept safe, since they must last her a lifetime without him. So great was her sense of his loss that words were inadequate to express her memory of him and language seemed too fragile, only a "slender thread," to sustain the weight of her immense mourning.[47] Yet the loss of George Meredith seemed to provide temporary reconciliation for mother and daughter.[48] Perhaps with the removal of the disputed male the women could finally make their peace. Webb's recovery from this second bout of illness was slow, though less slow than before. Her already intense introversion increased. In an effort to overcome Mary's shyness, friends of her mother talked Mary into attending Literary Society gatherings and it was at a gathering of this group, in the first year after her father's death, that Mary met Henry Bertram Webb.

He had graduated from St. Catherine's College, Cambridge, in 1907 and had returned to Shropshire to teach at a preparatory school near Meole Brace where his father, a retired physician, had recently bought a house. Henry had heard of Mary. Ethel Webb, his sister, had become friends with Muriel Meredith, who described her eldest sister to Henry. When Henry and Mary actually met, they discovered that they had a great deal in common. Both had literary interests and both shared an enormous love of nature,[49] a love based not so much on the natural sciences as on an understanding of nature as an aesthetic system to be experienced rather than scientifically analyzed.

Henry's pleasure in books and nature must have reminded

Mary of George Meredith, and like her father, Henry was a scholar and teacher and took pleasure in writing. In 1911, Henry Webb's book of philosophic essays on nature, *The Silences of the Moon,* was published by The Bodley Head. Two years earlier, Mary's first short story, "The Cedar Rose," had been published in *Country Life,* but her own nature essay, "The Scallop Shell," was rejected and was not published until it was included in *The Spring of Joy* in 1917.

Despite their shared interests and perceptions, the relationship between Henry and Mary might well have struck others as curious if not mismatched. Mary was nearly five years older than Henry: she was over thirty, and she still bore the physical signs of her previous illness, still suffered from its effects. Henry was twenty-six, attractive, and vigorous. He was outgoing and friendly and a stimulating classroom lecturer, while Mary's shyness remained unmitigated. But the similarities overcame the differences, and in June 1912, the two married.

The wedding plans that might have been an occasion for rejoicing provided an occasion for both mother and daughter to take to their beds with their particular forms of illness. In Wrenn's judgment, Alice Meredith's illness was the product of frustration with her daughter's casual approach to the social proprieties an engagement and wedding demanded. The bride made no preparations for a wedding gown; she chose as her single attendant not a sister but the gardener's young daughter; and she had invited seventy guests but would not say whom.[50] And, in fact, Alice Meredith was soon to learn the very worst: the seventy guests were nearly all residents of Millington Hospital, the local almshouse. Alice was to observe exactly the sort of spectacle she feared as Winifred Dowsett, the three-year-old bridesmaid, dragged an enormous red hassock into Holy Trinity, the parish church, and up the aisle, where she proceeded to climb upon it and sit as the bride, now recovered for the ceremony, and groom ascended the altar steps.[51] Mary's wedding plans and the actual ceremony and party of oddly mixed guests that followed may seem highly amusing, but part of our amusement most certainly comes from the knowledge of how unamusing the punctilious and socially aware Alice Meredith must have found the entire matter. One cannot help but think that Mary Webb's pleasure in her guest list and choice of bridesmaid arose from a similar understanding of her mother's nature, and an impish desire to annoy her. But her socially unconventional wedding plans also suggest Webb's growing tendency to identify herself, even in her happiest moments, with those beings, either animal or human, who could be considered society's downtrodden or nature's weakest. Having been physically stigmatized herself, she began to unite her fate with that of those marked by poverty, helplessness, disease, and the terrible isolation such alienation from the social whole can cause.

The illness Webb experienced just before her marriage was quite serious. She was weak and in pain, suffering from vertigo, severe migraines, and intense depression.[52] She allowed no one but Henry Webb to nurse her, an unconventional demand that could only add to her mother's displeasure.[53] The Merediths' usual doctor was away and a young doctor from elsewhere was called in. He prescribed a regimen of capsules filled with dried beef blood, a cure that, had she known the capsules' contents, she would surely have refused. Assured by Henry that the red matter was merely dried herbs, she took the medicine and began to improve.[54] The capsules may have supplied some iron and some of the vitamins and other minerals missing from her vegetarian diet, but they probably did nothing to change the nature of her disease. True to its fluctuating symptoms, the thyroid malfunction improved extremely rapidly, and Mary was a healthy and happy bride on her wedding day. The couple honeymooned in a cottage in the South Shropshire hill country, then left for Weston-Super-Mare where Henry would be teaching in the autumn term. With her move from Shropshire and her marriage at the age of thirty-one, Mary Webb's career as a novelist was about to begin.

The Golden Arrow

The Father's Lessons in Love

Probably everybody has a more or less concealed inner chamber that he [sic] hides even from himself and in which the props of his childhood drama are to be found. These props may be . . . quite simply the unmastered aspects of his childhood suffering. The only ones who will certainly gain entrance to this hidden chamber are his children. With them new life comes into it, and the drama is continued.

ALICE MILLER, *The Drama of the Gifted Child*

In Webb's first novel, her critics say, she attempted to re-create the warmly protective relationship she had with her father. George Meredith's death had caused his daughter a grief that found its only comfort through his re-creation in the character of John Arden, the mystical shepherd and perfect father of *The Golden Arrow.*[1] But her father's death had not been Mary Webb's first loss of him. She lost her father twice, the first time in 1900, on the morning when Alice Meredith returned to her proper place as mistress of the house. Meredith's death recapitulated this earlier loss and ended forever Webb's hopes of regaining the warmth of childhood intimacy. Thus, while the novel tells the story of an adult daughter's education in mature sexual love, that daughter nonetheless maintains a child's relationship with her father. The novel fulfills the early childhood fantasy of an all-protecting father who can at least ameliorate, if not actually rectify, the inequities of the world. Because his power to do so is unquestioned, important aspects of the world of female adulthood are noticeably absent in this novel. What *is* present is nurturing paternity; what is missing is oppressive patriarchy. Maternity's part in the growth of the daughter is well meant but ineffectual. Although this is a novel about women and love, marriage and birth control, pregnancy and abortion, infidelity and desertion, marital chastity and extramarital sexuality, there is no sense that such concerns are particular to the adult, sexual female. Family size and abortion are made matters of the heart rather than issues of larger implication—issues that result from men's control of society and its institutions and thus of women's sexual lives as well. What is important is that Deborah Arden learn her father's love lesson. Once that lesson is learned, Webb depicts all the problems that confront women in loving men as falling into perspective and happily resolvable. Love can overcome sexual inequalities—not by enabling a woman to end them but by enabling her to accept them as part of the human condition.

In her first novel, Webb depicts the father as the best adviser for a young woman who is questioning the nature of romantic love and the meaning of its demands on her still emerging identity. Because the daughter learns love through her father's instruction, she is educated in the joyful intricacies and paradox of mystical union. His lesson removes romantic love from its social and domestic context; for John Arden, romantic love is a transcendent experience and not a social construction. Had Deborah been tutored in love by her mother, Patty Arden, the daughter might have been taught the lessons of love's physical nature—that it is not spiritual heights but sexual intimacy which will shape the wife's future and that the growth of her soul might have to take second place to the growth of her children. John's lessons are aesthetic and mystical; Patty's would be practical. John's lessons, however, have little to do with the fact that marriage and subsequent maternity create conditions for women that are very different from those created for men with marriage and fatherhood.

In Deborah Arden, Webb creates a daughter for whom romantic love can exist apart from the dangers, pain, and loss of autonomy and youthful beauty that are the result of female sexuality's enactment in patriarchally structured marriage and motherhood. She is a daughter who finds her father's spiritual lessons, rather than her midwife mother's knowledge, more to her liking. She is a daughter who becomes both wife and mother, who emulates her mother, but who yet remains safe from the vulnerabilities that maternal emulation confers. Deborah lives with her lover before he is her husband, but she is not rejected by her family or criticized by her neighbors. She accompanies her sister-in-law to the abortionist, but is too innocent to understand the reasons for such a visit. She becomes pregnant but gives birth in so deep a psychic coma that she remembers nothing of the event. Through Deborah, Webb is able to affirm love as mystical union while denying its sexual nature and physical outcome. As in Adrienne Rich's poem, "Power," Webb would refuse the knowledge that the source of female power is also the source of female pain, that the value accorded women who learn to love and sacrifice is the source of their oppression.

* * *

The Golden Arrow was written in three weeks and completed in the spring of 1915.[2] Webb had begun some preliminary notes for the novel in 1912, during the first year of her marriage, when she and Henry moved to Weston-Super-Mare for Henry to take a post at a local school. With their move from Shropshire, Webb once again began to suffer from migraine attacks and from severe depression.[3] After two years, the couple returned to Shropshire and made their home at Rose Cottage, Pontesbury, only a few miles from Shrewsbury. At Rose Cottage the couple decided that they would both write, Henry essays and criticism and Mary poetry and stories, while trying to make their living by selling vegetables from their garden. Neither of them had any idea of the amount of labor, much less the sheer vegetable poundage, necessary to return a profit large enough to live on. There is an aura of play surrounding this entire undertaking; the couple were still honeymooning in a sense, still playing house rather than keeping house.

This return to the soil by middle-class people who were themselves never part of the soil originally is the perfect example of rural sentimentalism. The population of England's cities was increasing and the rural population was declining. Suburbs grew and began to encompass what once had been country lane and hamlet; village residents considered London's advantages, and farmers contemplated exchanging the plow and field for factory work and a flat. But a portion of the middle class sought country living—at least on weekends—and found preferable the vision of an England of hedgerow and greensward to that of the rapidly industrializing nation it had become. While village blacksmiths looked cityward, London accountants bought country cottages newly abandoned. Although Webb had never been a city dweller, neither had she nor Henry been farmers. The posture of the farmer was as artificial for them as was that of villager for those gentry who esteemed the provincial only insofar as it pertained to landscape rather than culture.[4]

It is interesting that the writing of *The Golden Arrow* coincides with Webb's return to Shropshire. The intense pace of her writing suggests the novel's existence as an imaginative whole. It would seem that she did not pause in her creation of the story, because it existed in entirety and needed only to be put down upon the page. She had returned to Shropshire as an adult, as a married woman. She had proved that she was loved and valuable; she had fulfilled the role expected of her. She had regained her earliest landscape, one she had walked with her father, and begun the first steps of maternal emulation. She was therefore the "good" daughter. What could be a better position from which to write a novel concerned with the parents' role in a daughter's romantic education?

As a first novel, *The Golden Arrow* is more filled with obvious autobiographical detail than any that will follow it. The landscape surrounding Rose Cottage is lovingly described; the trials of a newly married couple are chronicled; John Arden, *pater familias,* shepherd, and mystic, all biographers agree, is a representation of George Meredith. Since it is a first novel, it is not surprising that it is flawed; it is far too didactic, especially for modern tastes, often telling its readers what they should learn from events rather than letting readers discover such meaning for themselves. The characters are often a pastiche of idiosyncrasies, but their eccentricities are sometimes depicted with such a blend of cruelty and accuracy that comedy is the result.[5] The novel's tale is rather melodramatic and needlessly complex. In an attempt to underscore her theme—that love is the greatest human achievement but is learned only when the lover accepts the fact that pain and joy are integrally united—Webb doubled everything, giving each character its mirror opposite, each marriage its opposing reflection, even each farm its double. Good fathers are contrasted with bad ones, selfish motives with generosity, midwives with abortionists, and good shepherds with brutal dairymen. *The Golden Arrow* tells the story of the familial relationships between the Ardens—Deborah the daughter, John the father, Joe the son, and Patty the mother—and between the Huntbatches—Lily and her widowed father, Eli. It tells as well of the romantic relationships between Joe and Lily, who marries to escape her abusive father, and between Deborah and Stephen Southernwood, who persuades a rather reluctant but nonetheless loving Deborah to live with him before marriage but who is persuaded in turn to marry her. Stephen, selfish and immature and fearful of the confines of social institutions such as marriage, is contrasted to Joe, simple and kind but spiritually incapable of the passionate intensity that is the primary characteristic of Stephen's love. Joe loves Lily loyally and so cannot comprehend how deliberately she enticed him into marriage with her sexual allure. Lily is blond—as are all sexually attractive women in Webb's novels. She is pretty, shallow, and vain, capable of only the most selfish sort of love, unlike Deborah. Lily finds Joe's physical strength, his obvious adoration of her, and his protection from Eli's abuse electrifying. But she finds Joe's insistence on a large family a threat to her trim figure and soft hands. She wants to be known as pretty little Mrs. Joe Arden; Patty Arden's clearly maternal figure seems to her disgusting.

On his wedding night, Joe discovers that Lily intends that they live together as brother and sister. He spends the night in a chair, hoping that his young wife's seeming modesty will disappear with the familiarity of marriage. Deborah, meanwhile, succumbs to Stephen's desire and spends the night with him. Despite her mother's fears and unhappiness, she agrees to live with Stephen without marriage. John Arden makes it clear to his daughter that the lamp in the hall will always be lit for her each night, just as it has been; she will always be welcome at home. For Lily, Joe is too much the peasant; she prefers Stephen's good looks and manners and begins to make her interest known to him. Always restive with conformity to social dictates, Stephen is flattered by Lily's interest. One afternoon the two embrace and kiss. Trivial as the dalliance is, Stephen is overcome with guilt. Even more unbearable, however, is the imprisonment of his own marriage and he deserts his wife, who, unknown to him, is pregnant. Lily does not want children because of her selfish desire to keep her figure perfect and her hands soft; Stephen does not want Deborah to have children because of his selfish desire to have his wife all to himself. It is an unbreakable cycle.

Deborah, distraught at her abandonment, burns down their cottage and returns to her father's house, too emotionally broken to be fully aware of the birth of her child. Lily's marriage also has begun to falter and one night she gives in to Joe's importunings. Shortly after, she discovers she is pregnant and goes to the village herb woman for an abortificant. Deborah accompanies her, innocent of Lily's intentions, but repeats to her mother what she has heard and seen. Because Mrs. Arden is a midwife, she understands immediately Lily's plans and informs Joe. Joe confronts Lily and the two come to an agreement. Joe will not insist on six children, nor boast to Stephen and his neighbors about the number of children he will have without first consulting Lily. In turn, Lily agrees to have this one child; she has begun to realize that pregnancy will bring her pleasant attentions.

Lily and Deborah each finally has her child, Lily's named after Stephen and Deborah's after her father. John's tender ministrations, his nursing and his spiritual healing, cure Deborah. But when she walks in the hills one afternoon and meets Stephen, she is amazed to find that he still loves her. Their reunion is accomplished with Stephen's sincere apology and his hard-won knowledge that love entails responsibility. Deborah has also grown wiser and learned that love will be the cause of pain as well as joy. With the couple's acceptance of the paradoxical nature of love between the sexes, and with the peaceful if not ideal union between Joe and Lily, the novel's theme of love as a union of opposing forces is fulfilled.[6] Family and village life continue much as they always have; marriage unites both the generous and the petty in spirit; love is the great healer, transforming even the selfish into those willing to sacrifice self for the life of others: Lily for her child, Stephen for his family.

* * *

Not only is John Arden the hagiographic depiction of George Meredith, as Webb's critics suggest, and not only is the landscape of the novel that of her childhood's familiar topography, but in this tale John Arden is brought into the daughter's bedroom, as nurse, while Patty Arden is banished, at the father's insistence, to the kitchen. Webb creates the circumstances she had wished for when her own mother renounced her invalidism and re-entered family life some twelve years earlier: the mother's rule denied by the father's preference for a daughter whose psychic and physical need for his presence was a product of his own tutelage.

That her husband's presence in the sickroom is more valued than her own makes Patty Arden "wildly, concealedly jealous."[7] Patty is ill at ease with the stillness required during her nightly vigils over her daughter. Fidgeting and rustling and creaking in the old rocker, her mother only wearies Deborah's nerves further.[8] What is needed is more than the deft hand of the nurse; it is "the unskilled hand of a lover, the timeless gaze, the care that knows nothing of precaution or precedent."[9]

John Arden, of course, is the "unskilled" lover, not Stephen Southernwood, for in the fictive world of this novel, daughter and father form a bond as intimate as that of lovers. Watching Deb's semicoma, her father sits by her bed hour after hour, "silent and breathing out love. In his eyes lay the anguish of a great lover confronted with pain that he cannot cure."[10] Meanwhile Patty Arden often leaves her kitchen for the far end of the garden where she sobs as she contemplates the fact that her own ministrations disturb her daughter's peace. If she at times resentfully removes herself from her own kitchen so that her tears and sobs will not be heard, she is at other times literally banished to the kitchen from her daughter's bedroom. John invents reasons for her presence there, on one occasion suggesting he smells something burning.

Alice Meredith is re-created in a new form as the mother the daughter desired her to be, Patty Arden. Both mothers, in other words, the real one and the fictive one, are shaped and then disposed of. Deborah's preference for and need of her father is sanctified and fulfilled. Patty's well-meant but unwanted claims on her daughter—"She'll ne'er get right if he dunna give me a chance to nurse her"—are circumvented by John.[11] The maternal figure is made anew, warm and comforting; but she is then removed spiritually from participation in the tender relationship between father and daughter by her lack of understanding of her daughter's needs, and she is removed physically, by her hurried descent into the kitchen.

The father is regained and the mother banished; the bedroom offers the tableau of recumbent daughter and ministering father: the Freudian shape of the story is blatant. Blatant too is the daughter's final achievement of revenge, because the world of the novel is certainly the world prior to Alice Meredith's resumption of her role as wife and mistress of the house. But it is also, at the same time, the enactment of the daughter's power to remove her mother even after she had descended the stairs from her bedroom, positioned herself once again in the center of the family, and regained her husband. In that real world, Webb the daughter could do no more than take ill, lying on a sofa in the middle of the parlor, the observed and observing martyr to her mother's power. In the fictive world, Webb the writer can perform what Webb the daughter could not: this time it is the mother who must relinquish her position and the daughter who remains. This

time, the father connives with the daughter to banish the
mother to maintain their intimate relationship.

But the mother must relinquish more than her part in the
relationship between husband and daughter. She surrenders
her ability to influence her daughter, her ability to shape her.
Deborah is her father's daughter. It is John's love of solitude
and silence that Deborah inherits, rather than Patty's energy,
which makes contemplation and even solitude quite impossible for her. Father and daughter often watch the change of
landscape caused by clouds and weather; both find some im-
perfectly articulated meaning in the wild vista. The Devil's
Chair, a ridge of towering black quartzite which stands above
the rest of the hills, is the site where Stephen will insist that
he and Deborah build their cottage. It has been a constant
point of observation for father and daughter. John links the
preternatural evil of the Devil's Chair with the hope-filled
legend of *The Golden Arrow*:

In time gone by the lads and wenches in these parts was used to go
about Easter and look for the golden arrow. It met be along of them
getting sally-blossoms for Palm Sunday as the story came; but
howsoever, they was used to go. And it was said that if two as were
walking out found the arrow they'd cling to it fast though it met
wound them sore. And it was said that there'd be a charm on 'em,
and sorrow, and a vast of joy. And nought could part 'em, neither
in the flower of life nor in the brown winrow. And the tale goes
that once long ago two found it in the sally-thickets down yonder.
And they came through Slepe singing, and with such a scent of
apple-blow about 'em as never was. . . . And they went like folks
that want nought of any man, walking fast and looking far. And
never a soul saw them after.[12]

In telling the legend of the Golden Arrow, John Arden joins
pain and love and describes the love-charmed couple as no
longer part of their usual world. This is not a description of
a romantic infatuation that renders the lovers oblivious to
those around them. This is a description of love which suggests that true lovers—those who experience love as transcendent—no longer look to this world but seek beyond it.
John's ability to accept the presence of paradox will heal

Deborah and mend her broken marriage. It is the father's vision, rather than the mother's, that shapes Deborah's life and marriage. But Deborah does, in the end, emulate her mother's role: she marries, has a child, is content at the novel's end with her domestic role. She does not chafe at wifehood or maternity. Despite her initial agreement to live with Stephen without marriage, and despite the break in their eventual marriage, she follows in her mother's footsteps. Deborah, unlike Lily, is the good daughter. Just as Patty gives her treasures "without a second thought"—offering Lily her favorite tea cups as a wedding present—so too Deborah's greatest virtue is her generosity.[13]

Webb the author through Deborah the daughter regains the father, reshapes and then banishes the mother, even as she enables herself to fulfill the mother's expectations for a daughter who would emulate her. Webb achieves all she could want: she can possess the father, control her mother, and *still* be a good daughter. Webb the daughter did not manage as well. She was childless when she wrote *The Golden Arrow,* and she was to remain so. It was a state that her biographers conjecture caused continual personal unhappiness. Although Webb's marriage was quite happy at this time, she was certainly a less than conventional picture of the ideal wife in her overwhelming passion to write, in her insistence on farming as an occupation, and in her complete disregard of domestic chores lest they interrupt her writing.

This is the world Webb's desire created. She can possess not only the world she lost with George Meredith's death, but also the world she relinquished with Alice Meredith's return. She can regain what she once had; she can create what she had not. The reality she would create anew is a narrow one, one of personal, rather than social or cultural history. The world beyond the Meredith farm, the larger society of which the Ardens are only a part, remains unchanged—in fact, remains unmentioned. Yet that world and its social expectations directly impinged on the Meredith family, and in *The Golden Arrow* directly influence character and plot.

The Golden Arrow re-writes history. The practical Patty Arden is the mother Webb would wish for, not simply because her warmth is an antidote for Alice Meredith's aloof maternity, and not only because the kindly Patty would want to fulfill her daughter's needs, even at her own expense. Patty Arden's midwifery, her intimacy with the lore of barns and breeding, her easy humor about the earthier side of life ally her—safely—with the realms of maternal sexual knowledge. And since she can be denied access to her daughter, since the father makes that denial possible, the daughter can be spared the sexual knowledge the mother would impart.

Perhaps not as the child of fourteen she was when her mother first took to her bed, but certainly as the woman she was at nineteen when her mother resumed command of the household, Webb must have been aware that the fact that her mother stopped having babies was related to becoming an invalid. Webb may have concluded that illness prevents conception, either because of a husband's consideration for his wife or because of the nature of the infirmity itself. But another possible interpretation, one that does not deny the first and can coexist with it, is that for her mother illness was preferable to pregnancy—that the results of female sexuality are to be avoided if possible. Mary Webb may not have viewed her mother's illness as a form of birth control, though it may have been, but Mary may have understood that invalidism as a means of escape from sexual activity itself. She would associate her mother's illness with female sexuality's vulnerability. Knowledge of such vulnerability was something the still newly married Webb of 1912–14 would prefer to deny, evade, refuse. A character too closely depicting the real Alice Meredith might be too terrifyingly powerful a figure, even in fiction, to banish. But the gentle, sympathetic Patty could represent the mother—and *she* could be physically and emotionally divorced from her daughter's sexual growth, silenced from telling what the daughter would not choose to hear.

John becomes the center of the world in this novel. It is not surprising that such a father—one who can make the world right—takes on the qualities of deity, not of God the Father

but of Christ the Son, since God the Father is too closely
associated with the rigidity of moral dictates, while Christ
the Son is associated with gentleness and love, with the
simple things of the world. There is something more in this
re-creation of George as John the Good Shepherd rather than
John the Father/God. To re-create George as the godly Father
would be to look to the larger world, and that is precisely
what Webb does not want to do; to re-create George as Christ
the Son is to circumscribe the locale of his power, to pinpoint
it to the human heart rather than to the social whole. Webb
will go even one step further and substitute for the Christian
metaphor of the Good Shepherd the Welsh mythological figure of Cariad, the Flockmaster. She thus positions John in the
more pantheistic light; spiritual healing is still a matter of love
and sacrifice, but now that lesson can be learned out of doors,
in meadows and while contemplating mountains. Love, in
other words, can exist apart from religious, moral, or social
constructions. John the flockmaster can teach his daughter to
love free from social constraints. The father's lesson is mystical, born from his union with the world of nature, not the
world of social ritual. He acknowledges human suffering and
love's pain, but he does not particularize such suffering as
having specific form for a woman. John teaches universal love
rather than romantic love and all it entails for a daughter.
While John can wax eloquent and lofty in his rough, country
diction about the mystical paradox of love's freedom and responsibility, he cannot address the dualism which is socially
created for women in love: that the pleasures of sexuality result in the duties of often endless maternity; that the daughter
who gains wifehood loses selfhood.

John's lessons in love are appropriate for the prepubescent
daughter but not terribly useful for the mature woman, and
it is not surprising, therefore, that this novel employs Webb's
childhood landscape. Glen Cavaliero points out that the rural
world of The Golden Arrow lacks any real sense of an England
beyond Shropshire, that is, of an encroaching industrialized,
socially complex urban world of which this landscape is only
a small part.[14] But to admit the presence of that larger world

would be to admit its adult concerns. In London, suffragists publicly debated "the woman question." England entered into a world war. The entire nature of rural cottage life underwent change, as a consequence of the availability of effective and safe birth control which freed women from domestic duties and enabled them to engage in part-time employment and improve their family's standard of living. But none of these events are even mentioned in the novel. Webb circumscribed her novel's world. This is the geography of desire and not of fact.

It is the father who keeps his daughter safe and teaches her love's proper lesson. His lamp guides her through a storm after Stephen has deserted her and she has burned their cottage. It is John who nurses Deborah during her breakdown and throughout her pregnancy. It is John for whom the child is named. John is paternity—the father as person—warm and protecting, rather than patriarchy—fatherhood as institution; he is a Christly figure of redeeming love while Eli Huntbatch is an Old Testament figure of power and wrath with his "plain living, his long prayers, his loud confessions of sin, his harsh treatment of himself and his unquestioning meekness to the God he believed in—a vengeful, taloned replica of himself. . . ."[15] John is "infinite compassion"[16] and "endless charity."[17] His eyes are "wistful with his long gazing into oncoming storms and unattainable beauty and the desperate eyes of his strayed and sick sheep."[18] John Arden's lamp leads his daughter home through threatening weather, and *The Golden Arrow* enables Mary Webb to return to the safety of her own now-lost father.

Webb's biographers' suggestion that her sanctification of the father occurs because of George's innate goodness is too simple. It is true that no other father in her novels will be so sanctified; the fathers of *Gone to Earth, Seven for a Secret* and *The House in Dormer Forest* are pompous and foolish at best and self-centered and neglectful at worst. Old Sarn of *Precious Bane* is brutal and produces a son who chooses to emulate him. But John Arden–like figures are nonetheless to be found in all those novels, transmuted, however, into lovers. Kester of *Precious Bane* is most clearly a Christ figure and is referred to in Prue's loving fantasies as "the Maister." Robert Rideout, the poet-shepherd, resembles John Arden in his love of nature though not in his need to dominate, and Michael Hallowes, whose very name suggests his association with the sacred, is clearly priestlike when he ritually tests Amber's love and devotion. Webb's continued creation of these father/lovers suggests that personal history necessitated casting significant male figures as saviors who, in each case, circumscribe the world of the daughter/lover. She does not look to the larger world; she looks solely to them, and she discovers in each case that her real happiness consists in this single preoccupation. This is the outcome of the father's lesson in love. Choosing the man/savior, she need not choose the world and society, and in forgoing the larger world, the daughter/wife forgoes singular identity. She becomes, as *In Seven for a Secret,* the herdsman's wife and her children's mother; the adolescent girl who would seek fame and glory is gone forever. Only Hazel Woodus of *Gone to Earth* insists that she will carry out her own will and refuses to immure herself in the parlor and bedroom and settle down with one man forever; she is chased to her death by a pack of dogs.

These lover/saviors offer refuge from the larger, real world, the world where marital chastity is an unhappy but nevertheless employed form of birth control, a world where abortionists not only possibly serve to even up the sexual double standard which entails that women suffer more than men, as Webb notes, but serve also as corrective to a social construction of female value as centered only on her biological reproductivity.

John Arden's lesson is that love entails mutual compromise; it is a gentle lesson, without bitterness or anger, and Deborah as the good daughter learns it through anguish, as Stephen does. Lily's fear of the loss of her figure through multiple births is, we are to understand, the product of selfishness, an interesting judgment in light of Alice Webb's maternal history. One suspects that more than Alice Meredith's pretty figure was at stake when she chose sustained infirmity, and one suspects, as well, that many women chose invalidism as a sanctioned form of marital chastity when other types of birth control were known, even among rural doctors, but perhaps not so well-regarded by women as pious and morally upright as Alice.

The re-creation of her father in John Arden allows Deborah the fictional daughter and Mary the real daughter to see their unhappiness in personal terms: love's lesson improperly learned. Happiness can be gained through personal growth and through the agency of love. Society and its dictates do not impinge on the lives of these characters. This is how Webb would have the world be, and she denies the discrepancy between fact and desire.

There remains, in other words, an unacknowledged reality, which, because its existence is not admitted, is also unchanged, unmodified. The characters of *The Golden Arrow* perform actions directed by personal desire and individual history. Lily's actions all stem from her selfishness, a result of her father's nature and the way he has raised her. Stingy, brutal, obsessed with the notion of woman as animal-like both sexually and intellectually, Eli Huntbatch has raised Lily without love or tenderness. Joe, on the other hand, is patient, plodding, and kind. He has learned his mother's "sexless solicitude" and her comforting practicality. Neither Lily nor Joe nor Deborah nor Stephen is portrayed as acting for any reason other than that of desire, and the shape of their desire is completely explicable in terms of biography. Never do the demands of a larger world—the need to fulfill the expectations of social conventions, or the demands of political reality, or the construction of society—determine behavior. It is, in fact, Stephen's mistaken belief that marriage and family are the demands of society and, therefore, artificially created responsibilities, rather than the natural result of human love, that is the catalyst for much of the novel's action.

Webb's need to modify reality, to shape the world to desire, results in the creation of particular aspects of the novel's plot: the principal character is a young female with two parents; she leaves home for love and ultimately to marry; she returns

home pregnant, abandoned, distraught, to be healed; she re-
unites with her husband. Webb's desire to shape a world must
also be the source of Deborah's moral opposite in the novel.
But what in Webb is satisfied by the creation of a character
such as Lily? Deborah allows the author to satisfy the need to
gain father and yet remain a good daughter; Lily enables the
author to deny the existence of those feelings that most def-
initely are not in keeping with good daughterhood. The creation of these two daughters reflects Webb's conflict concerning the nature of female love and its role in her growth.

Lily is all that a daughter should not be. She is angry; she
tries to kill her father. Furious with Lily's vanity and flirt-
ing—which result in her neglect of domestic duty—Eli cuts
off his daughter's hair. Eli later awakens to the sound of a rifle
shot and finds Lily aiming at him, intent on not missing this
time. Joe's arrival prevents this, but it is, ironically, the first
time that Eli is actually proud of his daughter.

Lily's blatant sexuality is the strongest motivating force in
her character. She is curious, desirous of male attention, both
pleased with and adept at using the power of her beauty. Yet
she is also hypocritical and morally self-righteous, loudly
proclaiming her own lack of interest in all matters concerned
with the physical side of marriage. She demands a chaste
marriage, but is nonetheless willing to initiate an affair with
Stephen, whom she considers by far the better catch. She is
a bully and a snob, enamored of the "picturesque: she begins
to contemplate herself in the cozy setting of kitchen shelves,
cupboards, clean paint and flowers. She has a vision of the
vicar's wife alluding to her as 'Joe Arden's pretty wife who
makes such good jelly.'"[19] She spends Joe's tiny income on
trinkets, admiring bright, cheap things.

But Lily's greatest fault is that, unable to love, she does not
want children, and she will use any means to continue her
childless state. Lily is wrong in all ways. No aspect of her
character, no action, suggests that she has a good or noble or
even forgivable side.

Webb does, however, portray Joe's assumption of six children as thoughtless, and his comment—"chillun's what makes women happy"—as foolish and wrongheaded.[20] Joe should have consulted with Lily about her preferences on family size. Clearly critical, Webb states that "it was not considered decent to talk to a woman about any of the physical necessities of life except eating. A woman who was to give herself to a man and bear his children was not consulted in either matter. A tacit understanding was the nearest approach allowed."[21] It is not suggested, however, that Lily had the right to choose to remain childless. Although a man might be thoughtless and society's prudish conventions foolish, it was nonetheless wrong for Lily to try to avoid pregnancy and, failing at that, to seek to avoid actual maternity. Lily's fear of physical pain, her horror at the loss of health and beauty, her desire to continue just as she is—all are treated by Webb as evidence of innate selfishness.

Yet Webb does not appear to oppose abortion. It is, therefore, Lily herself, rather than her actions, who is at fault. The abortionist, Nancy Corra, lives in a hamlet where the Romans once mined: "Huge heaps of lead refuse rose in unwholesome whiteness, like mounds of rather dirty sugar, round the deserted mines."[22] These white mounds, like unclean breasts whose milk is unhealthy, suggest that the character, like her dwelling, is suspect. Yet Webb points out that for Nancy's "acknowledged patients"—as opposed to those women who come to her in the night—healing aid is well dispensed: "She prescribed with surprising efficiency; her cures were simple, often drastic, usually very sensible."[23] Nancy's home site is unwholesome, and her own person dirty, but her medicine is good. With her thick, gray hair hanging to her shoulders and her unpleasantly cunning mouth, Nancy's appearance is unusual but strikingly beautiful.[24] Her eyes are "keen, far-seeing, mysterious, sardonic . . . spacious enough for the wistfulness of a saint."[25] If Nancy Corra's herbal knowledge is from the devil, as Patty Arden suspects, it still can serve a good purpose. Webb suggests that it is not clear whether Nancy's "interference with natural laws"—abortion—was patently evil or whether "she helped to right the balance of punishment between the sexes for the sin of 'going too far.'"[26]

The feud between Patty Arden and Nancy Corra is not caused by professional competition; their professions are very much opposite. The feud between midwife and abortionist is between the helper of nature and the interferer, between the mother of clean breasts and nourishing milk and the destroyer of motherhood and despoiler of milk. That Lily, in her pregnant distress, consults the latter rather than the former is indication—whatever ambivalent questions Webb might pose concerning the "unmixed evil" of the herbalist's skill—that Lily's desires are unnatural. Lily's behavior is not that of a natural woman. Patty with her maternal solicitude and Deborah with her unbounded generosity are the proper models of womanhood. Like Nancy, Lily is soiled. Although some good may result from consorting with the devil, the source remains ultimately rotten.

Providing a portrait of the unnatural woman, Lily functions as Deborah's opposite, emphasizing Deborah's true value, and as a feminine counterpart to Stephen in his still immature and selfish state. Both are attracted to glitter, but Stephen loves bright things because they can conceal "the black depths below; Lily loved them because they were all in all to her."[27] Lily's mistreatment by Eli underscores the loving relationships between parents and children, father and daughter in the Arden family. But such practical functions are not the only reason for the creation of such a character. By creating Lily and associating her with unnatural womanhood, Webb allies *all* Lily's feelings with the unnatural. The fear of pregnancy and birth, fear of physical change and forced maturity, resentment at the loss of youth and freedom and beauty—all feelings any woman considering pregnancy might experience—are made wrong. Such feelings do not exist in the natural woman, the good woman. By associating such feelings with Lily and never with Deb, and by further associating Lily with Nancy Corra's unwholesome hills, the fear of pregnancy and maternity is banished from the world of good daughters. Of course, one does not banish what does not exist; rather one displaces what is already there. Thus Webb creates a Lily so that a Deborah does not have to deal with emotions like fear and anger and self-interest. Like the paschal lamb, Lily bears the "sins" of the Deborahs of the world. A bad daughter is created so that a good daughter can exist. The character of Lily enables Webb to give existence to selfish, resentful, childish, and even murderous longings, but still remain a good daughter. Through Deborah, Webb can create the good daughter she longed to be. Through Lily she can exorcise—and punish—the bad daughter she feared becoming. Deborah's marriage to Stephen will flourish; they will be physically and emotionally happy. The two will achieve the sort of sexual and spiritual bliss that best characterizes medieval mystics, untouched by, even enhanced by, whatever agony life will necessarily bring:

Stephen would belong to the small company of men who hold the world back from the beast—the self-givers, the lovers, in whom the flesh and the spirit burn together with a steadfast flame, and light the earth. But he had so much to unlearn, to give up, to suffer. He was like the mass of stone that is to be a great statue, and how long the statue would be in the making none could say.[28]

Deborah has married a man above men. Lily remains married to the loving but rather doltish Joe.

Webb has created a past self to her own specifications, a self without the negative emotions of selfishness and resentment, and even fear. But she also creates a character who embodies those abhorred emotions, who can clearly be labeled as "wrong." The unacceptable is displaced and therefore can be expressed; the displacer is purified and the object of displacement vilified. By creating Lily, Webb brings into the world of the novel the concrete world of social and political concerns that would be absent if the story were concerned only with Deborah.

Deborah Arden's struggles with love and marriage, the lessons she must learn, are abstracted from an historical and sociological context. Deborah's story is about Love, about how Love conquers all things; it is, in a sense, paradigmatic rather than realistic. Deborah's struggles are far from the world of Margaret Sanger, overcrowded cottages, painful pregnancy, butchered births, and economic struggle. Hers are the eternal struggles of the human heart: love and loss. But Lily's struggles are those of the female body—a body in a world which, like Webb, attempted to ignore woman's physical struggling in the world of romance. That such struggle existed was not denied but was made "unnatural," because natural women would welcome childbirth. True and womanly Love would calm such struggle. Love and the desire to remain childless were antithetical in the conventional world of Victorian and Edwardian morality—and in the world of *The Golden Arrow.*

Webb's unwillingness to consider the possibility that a woman could marry and not want children might certainly be a product of her own childless state. But it is also, most certainly, a product of her refusal to admit into this fictional world of her desire particular facts of female life. Webb re-creates the past self and world of desire but she does not re-create the present, adult world of social and sexual complexity. Having regained the father, she must affirm the patriarchy; having banished the mother, she can now affirm the maternal. Webb would change autobiographical past; she would restructure her family, but not society. Lily's "sin" must be in not loving; to associate her actions with any external factors, for example, to suggest that there might be a real basis for Lily's fears of childbirth, was to admit that society and not just the individual was at fault. And if society were at fault, then the desired world could never be attained, could never be created; Love, then, could never conquer all.

Thus, although a segment of the world is modified through the fiction of the novel, a very significant portion is not. Webb creates the personal past as she would have it be, but she leaves untouched the larger world of the past—just as she leaves quite literally out of the picture of the world of *The Golden Arrow* that landscape which cannot be viewed from the hill of John Arden's cottage. While Webb is able to create and sustain a fiction so as to satisfy desire, she cannot see and accept desire's nonconformity with the real world, the world that does not match desire, that even hinders desire's achievement. She refuses to see the novel's world as fictive and not, therefore, attainable, and thus need not accept the real world—and its deficiencies—as untouched by the force of her desire.

Such a charge is not one of ethical failure, nor was Webb any more marred psychologically than the average, literarily productive author of any period. The charge, if that is even the proper term, is a literary-critical one, one made to explain the curious and obvious fact that this novel, as well as those which are to follow, details the lives of women as they learn to love men, yet neglects utterly those important realities that determined women's lives and most certainly determined her own. Webb clearly intends her novels to teach us something about the nature of love between the sexes and between parent and child, but she attempts to do that teaching through the creation of a world which has very little resemblance to one in which her readers learn and love. She fails to create the world of our own painful experiences precisely because she, too, has not learned how to love in such a world except by the denial of the validity of her own emotions and experiences, and by the denial of the real world of historical and sociological fact as the context for her lesson. The only way in which the love that she values can exist is through the creation of a world that does not exist. She teaches us to desire that which we cannot have except by fabrication, and she herself refuses to accept the world that is not a product of her fabrication.

Limited in her own authority because she was female, Webb created a world in which woman, free from society, had the means to achieve her own happiness. By placing the power for happiness completely within the individual, Webb made woman mistress of her own destiny. But to deny society's role in defining the nature of female happiness is to neglect the fact that both "woman" and "happiness" are socially constructed terms whose meaning is dependent on the culture's gender rules, which insist that womanhood and happiness are achieved through marriage and maternity—through wifely and maternal love. A woman could make herself happy if she loved; she could therefore cause her own unhappiness by refusing to love. Since woman has the power for happiness, there is little need to struggle against extraneous social forces. The cessation of that struggle, the acquiescence to the passive pose, is reflected in an early poem by Webb entitled, appropriately enough, "Safe":

> Safe from the world's long importunity—
> The endless talk, the critical, sly stare,
> The trifling social days—and unaware
> Of all the bitter thoughts they have of me,
> Low in the grass, deep in the daisies,
> I shall sleep sound, safe from their blames and praises.[29]

In a sleep nearly like death, Webb would escape the demands of society. Webb would sleep, unaware of the social evaluations and forces that surround her. Such escape is possible in sleep, but not in dreams and not in dreams' other form, fiction. In both, the world of fact returns, reshaped, coded, symbolized, transformed. In *The Golden Arrow,* Webb attempted to create a world safe from the fact that romantic love is not a personal and natural emotion, an impulse of the heart, but an institution. She created a world safe from the fact of female contingency, safe from the fact of the female body's unique vulnerability. In the world of *The Golden Arrow,* love is the only correct choice a woman need make, and once made, once she loves thoroughly and selflessly, all problems disappear.

Thus Webb will continue to write novels in which daughters become wives and often mothers, and she will punish daughters who seek to escape this destiny. Such daughters will be depicted as morally flawed, like Lily, or will have to die, like Hazel of *Gone to Earth.* Webb will, in other words, create daughters who are not what she is: daughters who are never successful artists, never successfully rebellious. She will create female characters who, in their acceptance of society's definition of love, in their emulation of their mother's role, in their domesticity and maternity, in their joy of self-sacrifice, become the daughter Webb desired to be yet chose to refuse to become.

3

Gone to Earth

The Untaught Daughter

A woman writing thinks back through her mothers.
VIRGINIA WOOLF, *A Room of One's Own*

In *The Golden Arrow,* Webb created the good mother and banished her—not cruelly, but to the kitchen—and kept the nourishing father for herself, first as attendant in the sick room, then in the form of an eponymous child, and finally in the person of the returned Stephen Southernwood who clearly has the potential to achieve John Arden's spiritual growth.

In her second novel, *Gone to Earth,* neither mothers nor fathers fare so well. Parents as well as surrogate parents fail utterly in their tasks of protection and instruction for life. Nor does Webb create other figures, as she did with Michael Hallowes of *The House in Dormer Forest* or Robert Rideout of *Seven for a Secret,* who successfully substitute for parental neglect and provide the missing love and safety. The father figure in *The Golden Arrow* was sanctified and given the power to "save" his daughter when even her mother's ministrations would have failed. But in *Gone to Earth,* and in the novels that follow it, fathers will not be so forgivingly depicted. The rage Webb must have felt toward her father's acceptance of his daughter's banishment and his wife's return—and even Webb's probable anger at his inability to protect her from Alice Meredith's cold criticism—finds literary expression in the creation of weak, fumbling, loud but impotent, and even brutish fathers, while male lovers become increasingly more Christly, more and more like John Arden. It is as if Webb were finally able to lay blame on the male parent, now that her first novel has exonerated him. But having still the desire to hold on to the childhood idealization of the father, she must create other male figures who can embody that earlier vision. She will, in her last three novels, place some blame on paternal figures who cannot give their daughters the means for independence and growth, but she will also create nonparental male figures who, at the novels' conclusions, seem to offer such promise.

Gone to Earth, like *The Golden Arrow*, was written with intense urgency. According to Coles, Webb wrote day and night, often not sleeping for long periods of time, with mounds of paper and pages in no particular order littering the floor.[1] Such frenetic activity could, of course, be the product of Graves' disease whose "thyroid storms" might account for both the energy and the impulse to work at such ceaseless speed. But her single-minded devotion to writing might also be generated by the immediacy of her anger, the renewed presence of her childhood emotions triggered into creative consciousness.

In the summer of 1916, Henry Webb was appointed to a full-time teaching post in Chester. The position provided a modest but needed regular income; he could now pursue his own scholarly activities. Henry shared his wife's enthusiasm for nature, but the constant need to hoe and sow and plow and reap if food was to be put on the table was not compatible with his academic interests.[2] The major drawback to his new position, however, was that the Webbs had to live in Chester during the week and could return to Shropshire only on weekends. There they lived in a small, remote, and less expensive cottage, The Nills, which they had rented in 1914 when "the difficulties of wartime living" forced them to resign tenancy of Rose Cottage.[3]

After George Meredith's death in 1909, Alice had sold Meole Brace and returned to Chester where she had lived before her marriage. During the week the Webbs now lived with Alice Meredith and Olive, the youngest Meredith daughter. In the early years of the Webb marriage, contact between mother and daughter had been minimal. Alice visited the couple only on rare occasions, making it clear that she disapproved of her daughter's disorganized housekeeping, but with the move to Chester, the women could not help but be in one another's way.[4] Wrenn states that there were frequent scenes, followed by hysterical tears, as mother and daughter fought their way through the months.[5] Mary's food paranoia returned. Weekends at The Nills provided some relief, but it was clear to Henry Webb that the Chester situation could not continue. In the spring, he resigned his position at The King's School and took a post at The Priory School in Shrewsbury for the following autumn. The couple returned to The Nills for the summer and began to plan to build their own cottage on Lyth Hill, near Shrewsbury but still in the country.

Webb's critics, noting that *Gone to Earth* was written during the war years, have viewed the novel as reflecting its author's perceptions of Europe's turmoil. Henry Webb had been kept from the army because of his poor eyesight, but two of the Meredith brothers were in France, and reports of the carnage on the Western Front were frequent and terrible. Newspapers carried the names of the dead and missing; the wounded began to return home. Mervyn, the youngest Meredith brother, was to return with part of his jaw shot away. One source of the conflict between Alice and Mary was Alice's utter lack of concern for the welfare of her sons in the war and continual comments that made clear her appalling lack of knowledge about the war.[6] Coles attributes Alice's insensitivity to a "tight self-centredness" which responded to the dangers of war with the casual dismissal: "'Oh, they're all right—they're in the trenches.'" The remote location of The Nills could offer some relief from the visual reminders of the war, but Chester, with its munitions factory, the returned wounded, and the daily newspaper, kept the war always before the eye.[7]

Wrenn finds in *Gone to Earth* a "cry against cruelty," inspired by the war;[8] Coles considers the novel Webb's attempt to deal with her lifelong preoccupation with the relationship between good and evil.[9] Webb, spurred by the cruelty and inhumanity of the contemporary world, presents nature and an ever-green England as the sole remaining repositories of peace.[10] John Buchan, in his introduction to the 1928 edition of the novel, mirrors Coles' opinion. Reading the novel during the terrible days of 1917, Buchan sought and found escape in its depiction of an England filled with the familiar and recognizable.[11] The novel seemed so devoid of contemporaneity that Buchan placed its setting approximately fifty years earlier—1870 or so—despite a passage that clearly dates the novel's events as occurring after 1909.[12]

His error is understandable and underscores the contention of both Wrenn and Moult that the novel also has its genesis in earlier, childhood events, Webb's first experience of death. Wrenn recounts Webb's experience when she was eight or nine years old and her father had arranged to use a dead duck as a sketching model. Moult suggests that Mary's lifelong fear of her father's hunting beagles accounts for the novel's insistent move toward death and its violent conclusion.[13] Thus the biographers see the novel as mirroring its author's horrors of the war but also as rooted in far earlier experiences. The novel is not simply a passionate denunciation of violence against nature, but the self-absorbed depiction of Webb's sense of her own helplessness in the face of the inexorable. Hers is a helplessness as great as that of the forest's creatures in the face of human cruelty. This is a story of a daughter whose maternal inheritance and paternal neglect bring about her own death. While the dog pack forces Hazel to her death-fall, it is all the mothers and fathers of the novel who are responsible for her becoming the pack's prey. But parental culpability is a fact she would both present and deny. In *Gone to Earth*, unlike *The Golden Arrow*, the daughter cannot be saved. Webb allows this daughter to undergo the worst of fates, a reflection of that psychic part of herself she perceived as having been irremediably damaged years before.

As the grimmest of her stories, this is a novel in which death and human cruelty triumph. Neither love nor goodness nor innocence offer redemption. As such the novel is oddly contradictory, able to please such readers as Buchan but hardly presenting a perspective which offers the least solace. This novel, like her first, was little read and scarcely reviewed, news of the Western Front taking precedence over fiction in the public's interest. Wrenn states that Webb herself had only a modest interest in the novel after it reached print, a noteworthy and somewhat inexplicable fact since all her adult life Webb was hungry for recognition and not shy to claim it.[14] One explanation may be that *Gone to Earth* is so strong in its denunciation of maternal inheritance that Webb felt no further need to concern herself. Satisfaction had been found; repetition was not necessary.

The Golden Arrow was written in less than a month; *Gone to Earth* took only slightly longer. Both novels were published in the same year. Perhaps in part because of the speed of its creation, perhaps because she was no longer an apprentice writer, or perhaps because she had told the first necessary and most clearly autobiographical story and could now concentrate her energies on one for herself, *Gone to Earth* is remarkably unified. Its vision is consistent and intricately presented from the very first page, and it is a conscious vision of doom. The novel's intended effect is the demonstration of the devastating results of middle class morality on the physical and spiritual life of the sensitive and good. The novel excoriates as impure the overpiously hypocritical and the sexually prudish. It demonstrates how notions of sexuality as bestial result in marriages in which spiritual love is never allowed to mature to its fullest expression, and in relationships in which the merely carnal can never develop into the spiritual. The fate that unfolds is that of an innocent and pure Hazel in the grip of society's sanctimonious morality; in the world of *Gone to Earth,* when the pure meet the impure, the impure triumph since society's approval stands behind them. Hazel is doomed because she is "natural"—and therefore good; that is the novel's consistent and hopeless vision.

This is, however, a highly self-pitying perception of the world. Those who claim that the sensitive must always suffer, that the innocent are too good for this earth and so must be destroyed by evil, that what is fine will be smirched by what is corrupt, place themselves on the side of the angels. And in creating the tale of the suffering saint the author narrates the story of herself as victim. Hazel Woodus's suffering is most revelatory of Webb herself. Hazel is Webb's attempt to depict one aspect of the daughter she would be, the daughter who can live apart from social constructions of femininity. But so fragile and vulnerable is this figure within the context of society and morality that she dies. Webb's daughter cannot survive because women *must* live in the world of patriarchy; that is their fate.

Thus the novel enables Webb to portray the fate of daughters who inherit the mantle of weak, unhappy mothers. But so terrible was that fate that Webb had to find some anodyne. And so she makes the suffering daughter into a saint and focuses the blame for her suffering on those whose insensitivity is so great that it is nearly evil incarnate. The daughter's helplessness is sanctified; parental responsibility for the daughter's suffering is partially deflected, and institutions rather than individuals can be blamed. In *The Golden Arrow* an individual could control her own fate and was responsible for her own unhappiness. But in *Gone to Earth*, Webb absolves the individual and tries to focus blame on the social institutions of church and marriage. Hazel's parents, and those who function as her surrogate parents, play large roles in helping Hazel meet her bloody end, but they are not, themselves, made the cause of her doom. While a strong mother or helping father might have changed the nature of her fate, it is ultimately the stultifying demands of marriage and the loveless morality of religion that doom her. Burdened by her pregnancy, Hazel cannot run for safety in the forest, nor can she find refuge in society.

★ ★ ★

Hazel Woodus has not so much been raised by her widowed father, Abel, as allowed to grow. She is unlettered, uncultured, ignorant of the feminine arts of sewing, cooking,

cleaning, and gardening, and, still worse, untutored in even
the most basic Christian beliefs. Maray Woodus, her mother,
was first attracted to Abel because of his harp-playing—Abel
earns his meager living by making coffins and funeral wreaths
and by playing at wakes and weddings—but finds herself unable to accept the imprisonment of marriage. A Welsh gypsy,
she hated cottage life and marriage; motherhood curtailed her
freedom further. Maray loves her child, but remains unsatisfied.

> She was a rover, born for the artist's joy and sorrow and her spirit
> found no relief for its emotions; for it was dumb. . . . All the
> things she felt and could not say, all the stored honey, the black
> hatred, the wistful homesickness for the unfenced world—all that
> other women would have put into their prayers, she gave to Hazel.
> The whole force of her wayward heart flowed into the softly beat-
> ing heart of her baby. It was as if she passionately flung the life she
> did not value into the arms of her child.[15]

Maray is utterly powerless to express her deepest needs,
much less her profound despair. She attempts, early in her
marriage, to learn to play her husband's harp; unable to draw
any music from it, she can only run her hands uselessly across
the strings. She can attain no satisfaction for her own desires;
there is no available means of expression. Her only utterance
is in the being of her baby, Hazel. The daughter thus becomes
the maternal self extended.

Patty Arden was not even a vague replica of Webb's
mother. Neither is this gypsy mother. Patty Arden's earthy
vigor and practicality were the exact opposite of Alice Meredith's infirmity and piety; Maray Woodus is diametrically
opposed to all that the Alice Merediths of Edwardian England stood for. As a gypsy, Maray is alien to her community.
She feels fettered by her marriage, longs with frustration for
a means of self-expression, loves her daughter but not maternity itself, and places her faith in pagan charms. It is in keeping with her character that when she dies she requests to be
buried in the Callow, amid the larches, rather than in the confines of the churchyard. Patty Arden's exemplary maternity

makes it right and natural that Deborah emulate her; there is no good reason for the daughter of such a woman to refuse to imitate her mother. But Maray Woodus is an example no daughter would be expected to follow. She could hardly demand that her daughter follow in her footsteps and become a wife and mother. With a mother such as Maray, a daughter is free of the burden of inculcation of the maternal role, hence free to become herself.

A strong, happy mother can create a daughter who sees no threat in emulating her mother's life. While Susan Peck MacDonald suggests that such mothers offer so powerful a figure that they may protect daughters from undergoing the trials and errors necessary for maturation,[16] these mothers do offer models for happiness, even if that happiness is located only in wifehood and maternity. But the weak, unhappy mother has no viable model whatsoever to offer. The daughter is free to make her own errors, but is provided with no guidelines for achieving happiness. The weak mother can give her daughter only her own helplessness, her own dissatisfaction and victimhood—and the daughter who knows no other pattern will follow her.

When informed by her disapproving aunt of her resemblance to her dead mother, Hazel is initially pleased, but recants and states that she wants to be just herself, that she wants to resemble only Hazel and none other.[17] That cannot be. And the novel's opening, with its series of forbidding moments when Hazel is caught, static, in a threatened pose, in threatening light, assures us that Hazel is indeed Maray's daughter and will not survive. Hazel bathed in the blood-red twilight, bloodstained by a trapped rabbit she has tried to free, made gray and wraithlike by the dying day—all are portents of the bloodied, mutilated Hazel of the novel's end. With no model but her mother—made by her mother, in fact, into the receptacle for Maray's inarticulate longing—Hazel is powerless to endure.

Hazel's aunt, also an example of failed maternal protection, sets into motion the events that will kill Hazel. Walking back late on a stormy night because her aunt is jealous of her son's obvious interest in her niece and so will not allow Hazel to spend the night, Hazel meets Jack Reddin, who offers her a ride. Reddin is fascinated by Hazel's beauty, and he is free in his admiration. She readily accepts his offer to spend the night with him at Undern. Hazel's acceptance, and her admission that her father will not be concerned with her absence, are products of her complete innocence of all things sexual. The rabbit's blood indelibly staining her new dress suggests that such innocence is about to come to an end, whether with Hazel's complete understanding and agreement or without. Reddin quite obviously has sexual intentions in making his offer; Hazel quite obviously has none in accepting it. She is pleased that Reddin is a "gentleman" and squire and that he has a servant. She easily repulses his advances in the wagon, but is quite pleased to be complimented and told that she is pretty and that her hair is "abron"—auburn—rather than the bright red her father disparages.

But Hazel will not escape. Although she evades Reddin's advances that night, the rabbit's blood has stained her dress, rub at it as she will. And Reddin's kisses, though initially unwelcome, are inevitable—and fatal: "Reddin suddenly gripped the long coils that were loose on her shoulders, twisted them in a rope round his neck, and kissed her. She was enmeshed, and could not avoid his kisses."[18] It is her hair that imprisons her in Reddin's embrace; she is caught by her own body—caught as was the rabbit in its trap. Reddin's lovemaking has only been delayed, not avoided. Reddin, as much as Hazel, is caught in nature's web of birth, growth, and reproduction. It is "natural" that girls become maidens and maidens wives and wives mothers. This is a trap larger than that which killed the rabbit, but because Reddin is a brutal hunter of game and of beauty, it is a trap that will kill Hazel since she, like her mother, is helpless to escape. All things grow and reproduce, but because Hazel is caught before her growth is complete, she never matures and can only die.

* ★ *

Reddin's Undern Hall represents both the nature of its
owner and the larger process of humans as agents in the continuation of life. Even in May, when all around Undern is
lovely, green, and singing, it is a place in which "the influence
and magic were not good."[19] Like many of the houses in
Webb's novels, Undern carries within its walls the history of
all who have lived there, the horrors of all that once happened
there. It is as though the past still lives on, and Undern is the
repository of human history. Its windows at dawn and sunset
have a "sanguinary aspect, staring into the delicate skyey dra-
mas like blind, bloodless eyes."[20] The small insects dancing
in the heavy air of midsummer make the house's size seem
oppressive and their brief life makes it seem "infinitely old."
Undern Pool is "full of leaf shadows like multitudinous loll-
ing tongues, and the smell of mud tainted the air—half sickly,
half sweet." In the garden the cherries fall from the trees
"with the same rich monotony, the same fatality as drops of
blood" to lie under the "fungus-riven trees."

Undern is half-dead, necrotic, a rotting body whose mind
is fixed upon the dead past. Yet in the heavy somnolence of
the afternoon, the drowsing cattle, the bird-heavy trees and
the wilting day-lilies, "the very principle of life seemed to
slumber." Undern can be awakened from death because its
very decay suggests the possibility of new life. The scent of
its decaying fruit, of its elder blossoms and yew—even its
mud—are as "aphrodisiac" as some exotic narcotic.[21]

But if in its brooding sensuality Undern Hall promises life,
it also hints at cruelty. In the winter the yews wave like "funeral plumes and mantled, headless goddesses," and the wind
lashes the Pool's ice and the house's old walls "like beings
drunk with the passion of cruelty."[22]

Then those within were, it seemed, already in the grave, heavily
covered with the prison of frost and snow, or shouted into silence
by the wind. On a January night the house seemed to lie outside
time and space; slow, ominous movement began beyond the blind

windows, and the inflexible softness of snow, blurred on the background of night, buried the summer ever deeper with invincible,
caressing threats.[23]

The house is both body and tomb, both sensuality and cor-
ruption. Like Jack Reddin, Undern is the carnal body unredeemed by spirit; past deeds and human lives weigh down the
house as sin might the soul. In Webb's other novels, novels
that are optimistic, houses such as this burn down. It would
seem that they can never be completely redeemed by present
lives; those who dwell in them will be compelled to duplicate
the terrible pattern of the past. History will necessarily repeat
itself in these infected houses. They represent matter invested
with mind, but a mind obsessed with only what is long past,
long dead.[24]

Like Undern, Reddin possesses the potential for both life
and death. Although he is a character merely carnal at the
beginning of the novel, redemption is a definite possibility. It
is part of the novel's irony that Reddin first experiences feelings of love only after he has raped Hazel. Afterward, as the
two sit in the woods, Reddin's eyes fill with tears—not of
remorse so much as of grief.[25] He fights such feelings, however, and in the end it is his brutality that triumphs. The
tenderness that welled up after his rape merely translates into
a desire to marry Hazel and have her bear the future heirs of
Undern. He considers himself noble for so honoring her, and
is even a little fearful of this sudden tender consideration. His
usual way with women has been merely to take his pleasure
and leave when pregnancy inevitably occurred. Reddin's current mistress—if a term so suggestive of power can be used
for a role as powerless as this—is Sally Haggard, who has
borne his four children and who will be displaced as soon as
Hazel is installed as Mrs. Reddin of Undern Hall.

After Hazel's escape from Reddin's advances on that first
meeting, she returns home, but not before looking back at
Undern's windows beneath a sky "crimsoned for dawn." The
house appears to stare back at her with a "look of power and
patience," and Hazel senses that the events of the night before

have begun rather than concluded something: "She wondered
how she would feel if Reddin sudenly appeared at his window. And a tiny traitorous wish slipped up from somewhere
in her heart. . . . Almost she wished that Reddin had awakened" and prevented her escape.[26] Abel Woodus does not
mention her absence the night before, exactly as Hazel had
predicted to Reddin, but Abel does inform Hazel that her pet
fox, Foxy, has once again caught a chicken and that the next
time this happens the fox will be drowned.

The little fox is clearly Hazel's counterpart, both in its col-
oring and in its desire for freedom. Foxy is "unrepentant and
dignified" even in her transgressions against society. As Hazel
admonishes the fox and warns her of the danger of eating
another chicken, Hazel expresses her desire to live free from
human society, in some place where there are neither men
nor women. But even the little fox seems to doubt the possibility that "such a halcyon place existed in the world."[27]
Abel confronts Hazel while she is still upset over Foxy's possible fate and while Reddin's compliments and admiration are
still fresh in her mind. Abel teases her about her red hair, so
recently called "abron," and in her anger and confusion manages to persuade her to promise to marry the first man who
asks her. Abel feels he has won a victory, having first raised
Hazel's wrath and having then forced her to promise to do
something she has always sworn to avoid. As Hazel watches
her father build a coffin for a neighbor, she articulates the
realization she came to the night before—that she is mortal:

Hazel looked at the narrow box, and thought of the active, angular
man for whom it was now considered an ample house. "It seems
like the world's a big spring-trap, and us in it," she said slowly.[28]

Abel tells his daughter of a meeting at which he has been
asked to play and sing, and she turns from her contemplation
of the coffin and her own death and begins to sing and dance
feverishly. Abel and Hazel spend the morning practicing their
music and the afternoon cutting holly for the funeral wreath,
but Hazel cannot stop thinking of the events of the night
before. She thinks wistfully of the heavy green silk dress Red-

din had allowed her to wear, and of the dinner served in a dining room by a servant. And she imagines that Undern might provide a safe place for Foxy. Yet when she steps to the cottage door, the air is frosty and the landscape frozen, and she resolves not to go to Reddin even for a visit: "I'll stay as a be. . . . I wunna be his'n."[29] Fetching a cloth to try to clean her bloodied dress she finds she cannot; the stain remains, and "as long as she wore the dress it would be there, like the stigma of pain that all creatures bear as long as they wear the garment of the flesh."[30]

Her night with Reddin has awakened Hazel's curiosity and her vanity. It has awakened, as well, her realization that she is part of rather than apart from the human community. Though she would desert the world of men and women and live in safe isolation with her fox, she senses, as does even the animal, that she cannot do so. Her knowledge that she must someday die forces her to feverish gaiety, but even that is not enough to erase her memory of Reddin and his appeal. Hazel can will herself not to see Reddin again, and she can ignore her foolish oath to marry the first who asks, but the trap has already been sprung. Her realization of mortality is a realization that she, like all women, is subject to forces beyond her control. For Webb, those forces were biological: life demands reproduction. Hazel's insight signifies a developing maturity, but this single moment of realization is not powerful enough to provide the wisdom that might ensure her safety. She is, from the novel's beginning to its end, bound to the earth, enchained by it, "prisoner to it only a little less than the beech and the hyacinth—bondserf of the sod."[31] She is nearly without an unconscious. She is pure instinct. And if there is a positive core to the novel, it is the fact that Webb portrays human instinct as innately good. It is society that corrupts; the natural is pure—but helpless.

★   ★   ★

It is because Hazel accompanies her father to his musical employment that she meets the minister, Edward Marston, who falls immediately in love. He is shocked by Hazel's ignorance of Christianity, but taken by her vitality and beauty and awed by her tremendous innocence. He realizes that she is without guile or flirtatiousness. As she sings, her head wound with a wreath of violets, her hair in tendrils about her face, Marston hears something in her voice which he cannot understand but which he responds to nonetheless: "the keening—wild and universal—of life for the perishing matter that it inhabits."[32] What Marston responds to in Hazel is the very soul of nature, the echo of things beyond human reason— and this is most seductive since thus far Marston has lived a coddled and attenuated life. While he is sure that his mother will find Hazel a great burden as a daughter-in-law, Marston is aware even before the concert ends that he wants to marry Hazel. Although Marston has spent his life following his mother's conventions, and although her comments on Hazel's singing are hardly complimentary, for the first time in his life Edward acts without his mother's approval.

★　★　★

Hazel marries Edward Marston out of a sense of honesty rather than love; she fulfills her promise. This marriage to Marston could offer a safe and loving place for her growth. But, abandoned by her dead mother, neglected by her father, she has learned nothing to help her survive in human world, much less in the world of love and marriage. She has from her mother only a book of charms and gypsy lore, and the memory of Maray's oft repeated injunctions against marriage and maternity. She has from Abel a love of music and dance, but no real art. Had she at least inherited her father's talent, there would be her salvation. His power to express himself through his music, his success, his total ease with the dark places of his soul could counterbalance Maray's mute helplessness in the face of misery.[33] Hazel can sing, but only with pleasure and not with art; she can dance, but without form and simply as the expression of youthful vigor. Like some wild creature, Hazel has matured unsocialized. She is strong and vigorous and fearless of all things in the natural world, nor does she fear the village world's critical eye. Society's no-

tions of propriety are precepts she has never learned. She is
without deceit, so she cannot recognize that quality in others.

Hazel does not claim that she loves Marston; she gives no
evidence of passion for him. And Edward, sensitive to Hazel's
innocence, decides that they will live as brother and sister for
several years, until Hazel indicates to him that she would like
to be his wife. In the meantime, Edward hopes that Mrs.
Marston will become Hazel's mother, teaching her the domestic arts, helping her to learn the Bible, and showing her
the manners and behavior expected of a minister's wife. Were
such a marriage possible, could Hazel and Edward live together as innocent siblings under the kind tutelage of Mrs.
Marston, Webb suggests that Hazel might grow, safe and
whole. Edward's scheme is only initially successful. Though
highly disapproving of Hazel, Mrs. Marston does teach her
the rudiments of cooking and cleaning and housewifery. Hazel begins to enjoy some aspects of domesticity. She takes
pleasure in her garden, in her dainty clothes and clean body,
the fresh sheets of the cottage, and in her knitting as the three
sit before the fire in the evenings while Edward reads to them
from some devotional text. The embryonic Hazel begins to
mature. She begins to feel a dim desire to emulate Mrs. Marston, and considers with some vague pleasure the notion of
possible motherhood. The memory of Reddin and her fascination with his dark sexuality begins to dim. But Hazel's vision of future maternity is seriously flawed; it is a child's vision devoid of sexual knowledge. Nor is that knowledge
likely to come from Mrs. Marston. And it is a knowledge
that Edward seems to feel comes through some process other
than articulation. Neither surrogate mother nor surrogate
brother/real husband is willing to instruct Hazel in the physical activities that precede pregnancy. That lesson Hazel will
learn through rape.

The Marstons' chaste marriage cannot continue. Webb tells
us that nature abhors such a scheme, since it is the role of life
to beget itself, to reproduce and die. All living things must
reach sexual maturity, and human will has no choice but fi-

nally to bow to nature's imperative. After a time, Edward finds himself in a continual struggle with his desire for his wife. Each night he must battle with himself as he escorts her to her single room and bids her good night. He cannot make a move toward her because he believes that such innocence as Hazel's indicates a lack of sexuality. Edward equates sexual desire with sexual knowledge; therefore, he cannot believe that his own desires for his wife, expressed in even the tenderest of ways, would be anything but repulsive to her. Hazel could learn to love Edward but he would have had to teach her love's physical expression. What Edward does not know is that even as he resists his own desire, Jack Reddin sits outside the house, day after day, attempting to seduce her. Nor does Edward know that Hazel's awakening sexuality has begun to respond to Reddin's temptation.

Although Hazel cannot articulate the attraction Reddin has for her, and although she feels guilty about her continued fascination with Reddin while she is married to Marston, she is nearly powerless to fight off the process encoiling her. Had Edward only surrendered to his own desire and made love to his wife, Hazel would have loved him in return, and with all the passion of her nature.[34] But Edward resists nature, and in accepting the social myth that sexuality and innocence are in opposition, he brings about the chain of events that will culminate in Hazel's tryst with Reddin in the woods. On her marriage day Hazel had walked to the cottage wearing on her head one of Abel's wreaths, a funeral wreath bedecked with spring flowers. Dressed in white and singing with happiness, Hazel carried in disguise her father's gift of death.

Just as Edward could have taught Hazel the pleasure of mature love and sexuality, Mrs. Marston, were she a different person, could have given Hazel the wisdom and strength she missed from her own mother. Edward as brother could have become Edward the husband; Mrs. Marston, the mother-in-law, could have become Hazel's spiritual mother. But both fail, even though the potential for Hazel's growth within their household is initially present:

Hazel had never felt so like a child in its mother's lap. Her own mother had not made her feel so. . . . But now she felt cared for as she looked round the low room with its chair-bed and little dressing table hung with pink glazed calico. There was a text over the fireplace: "Not a hair of thy head shall perish."[35]

The Marston house, so carefully tended by Mrs. Marston, brings indoors the natural world Hazel loves and cannot live without. There are flowers in the bedroom. The garden's produce lines the kitchen walls; glowing, jewel-like bottles of jams and preserves shine in the evening's firelight. Flowers surround the door and walk, and blooming fruit trees can be seen from the windows with their tidy, white curtains. In the first days of the couple's marriage the house seemed a warm and lighted place of comfort in the midst of the wild landscape surrounding it on all sides. Although Hazel was still clumsy in her kitchen work, she was happy as she moved from interior to exterior, tending the garden, hunting berries, and learning to make her own, still-inept jars of preserves.

But the house that at first offered Hazel such pleasure is a testament to Mrs. Marston's adoration of propriety. Because Mrs. Marston loves her son, she is determined to do her best for Hazel. She will try to make her into an appropriate wife. But her notions of what constitutes appropriate behavior have nothing to do with love, nothing to do with human growth. For all her piety, it is matter and not spirit that Mrs. Marston worships. Nothing must be allowed to disturb the unruffled calm Mrs. Marston most values, a calm far more like death than like peace. Hazel comes to realize that the jams and jellies she so admires are not to be eaten, but merely displayed. Hazel is a disturbing presence in the house, a presence Mrs. Marston hopes will soon settle into quietude and become "part of the house."[36] Since Mrs. Marston has never become a full human being herself, she cannot help Hazel grow. Webb compares Mrs. Marston to an insect who builds a house not to grow in but to be enclosed by: "She worked like the coral insect, in the dark, as it were, of instinct unlit by intellect, and, like the coral insect, she raised a monumen-

tal structure that hemmed her in."[37] The maintenance of that
structure is the mother's part in continuing the patriarchal
constructions of family, marriage, and so-called domestic
bliss. Women thus become equated with things, objects; as in
the Sexton poem, they "marry houses." Such women exist
to perpetuate life and make it cozy and ordered and clean, but
they do not exist to live life. Mrs. Marston's desire is that
Hazel will become part of the structure; she wants Hazel to
become matter rather than spirit:

Hazel would be absorbed into the Marston family like a new piece
of furniture. She would be provided for without being consulted;
it would be seen to that she did her duty, also without being consulted. She would become, as all the other women in this and the
other families of the world had, the servant of the china and the
electro-plate and the furniture, and she would be the means by
which Edward's children would come into the world. She would,
when not incapacitated, fetch shawls. At all times she would say
"Yes, dear," or "As you wish, Edward." With all this before her,
what did she want with personality and points of view? . . . But
Mrs. Marston forgot, in this summing up, to find out whether
Hazel cared for Edward more than she cared for freedom.[38]

Like her son, Mrs. Marston is not aware that Jack Reddin
waits for Hazel just beyond the cottage doors, just beyond
the firelight.

Marston, his mother, and Reddin pay no heed to Hazel's
repeated statement that she wants to be neither wife nor
mother—that her own mother has warned her against these
roles. Hazel can be lulled by the comforts of the Marston
cottage, and she can be impressed by the decaying grandeur
of Undern. But neither the places nor their owners can
change Hazel's preference for freedom of the forest and her
autonomy in the woods. Just as Foxy, fed though she is, escapes again and again to raid the chicken coop, Hazel's instincts are for freedom and action. Foxy is a good fox but a
bad dog, Hazel explains to those who would punish the animal. The little fox cannot be expected to be other than what
she is, but society will attempt to destroy her since all good

foxes will continue to kill and eat good chickens, as much out of pleasure as out of need—such is the nature of the fox.

Hazel is trapped by nature and society, by her body and its sexual desires. Nature, Webb states, demands the abrogation of female liberty so that the race can continue.[39] Society demands that such abrogation take a particular form: marriage, housewifery, acquiescence to the male, domestic interment. Nature does not offer dispensations to daughters who refuse maternity; society does not change its expectations for daughters who reject its forms. Hazel is trapped because there is no way for her to be herself within society, while life apart from it is equally impossible. Like Foxy, Hazel will follow her nature, and like Foxy, she will be punished. As the weeks of her marriage go by, Hazel finds it harder and harder to follow Mrs. Marston's rigid schedule, more and more difficult to remain at home. Like Maray, her mother, Hazel is restive within the confines of domesticity. Reddin continues to watch her and tempt her to walk with him, and finally Hazel gives in. Hazel's growing intimacy with Reddin gives her knowledge of human passion. For the first time, Hazel begins to blush when she recognizes Edward's muted desire for her, but she cannot bring herself to respond to his timid statement that she should tell him if she ever desires that he become her husband instead of her brother.[40] Edward is foolish to wait for Hazel to express her sexual desire; he must take the initiative, writes Webb, because "even if a woman knows whether she wishes for a husband, she will never tell him so."[41]

But Reddin, for all his outspoken and crude passion, can never truly appeal to Hazel. He is too brutal, a huntsman who is stained by the blood of his prey. It is precisely because Reddin is a hunter that he desires Hazel. Her grace, her vitality, her independence drive him frantic with the need to possess her: "A pretty woman should not have that easy grace; she should have exchanged it for a matronly bearing by this time, and independence should have yielded to subservience—to the male, to him."[42] Reddin would tame and domesticate her; he considers Edward womanish and not worthy of her. He is sure that he can offer her a better life than she now has with the minister and his mother.

Reddin's sexual advances and his kisses soon begin to haunt Hazel. Mrs. Marston has tried to stop Hazel from wandering in the woods, but this has only made her more restive. She is aware that Edward would not approve of her meetings with Reddin and feels guilty and confused. She would like to tell her husband and ask him to protect her. But because she senses that sexual impropriety is the worst sort of impropriety, she cannot broach the subject. Until she is actually raped, Hazel is ignorant of sexuality, although she has begun to understand desire. The refuge the Marston house has offered her—its wall-hung text promising safety—has no place for frank and free discussion of sexual matters. As Edward reads to his wife and mother from a religious text, Hazel comes to the conclusion that she cannot reveal Reddin's pursuit of her. Just as there is no room in the pious little book for real life, there is no room in the Marston house for truth:

The book was one of those affected by Mrs. Marston and her kind. It had no relation whatever to life. Its ideals, characters, ethics and crises made up an unearthly whole, which, being entirely useless as a tonic or as a balm, was so much poison. It was impossible to imagine its heroine facing any of the facts of life, or engaging in any of those physical acts to which all humanity is bound, and which need more than resignation—namely, open-eyed honesty— to raise them from a humiliation to a glory. It was impossible to imagine also how the child, which appeared discreetly and punctually on the last page, could have come by its existence, since it certainly, with such unexceptionable parents, could not have been begotten.[43]

One day, Reddin commands Hazel to meet him. She knows that she should resist but is nearly helpless: "It was as if someone had spun invisible threads between her and Reddin, and was slowly tightening them."[44] In an attempt to decide what she should do, Hazel consults her single inheritance from her mother, a book of charms, where she finds the Harper charm, to be worked before any major undertaking. If the undertaking were a good one, then the sound of harping

made by the silver folks with golden harps on a purple hill
would be heard. The next night Hazel secretly leaves the
house and waits in a hummock of the mountain where she
clearly hears the omen of the harp's music, and decides to
meet Reddin. What she does not know is that the music was
her father's: "Her bright galaxy of faery was only a drunken
man" returning from a summer festival.[45] Worse than the fact
that her belief in the fairy-world was no more than the byproduct of ale is the fact that she has made an irrevocable
decision because of her father's music and her mother's
charm. Although it is her parents who send her to Hunter's
Spinney, to Reddin, and finally to death, it is her husband
who sends her to another man's bed: "If he had listened to sex
. . . if he had for once parted company with his exacting
spiritual self, Hazel would have loved him."[46] Edward, Hazel
declares just before she leaves him for Reddin, is both her
mother and her father—he has attempted to give her love and
comfort; the pity is he is never her husband.[47] He has acknowledged his own physical desire, but never hers.

Hazel's remaining indecision is removed by her use of a
second charm. She places a clean chemise in the bracken overnight; in the morning there is a tiny blue petal in the garment's center. Sure that it is the promised fairy-flower, Hazel
takes it home, places it under her pillow, and dreams of Reddin. This is Hazel's final sign; now she must go to him. Had
she known that the petal was no fairy-flower but simply a
petal of blue milkwort she herself had loosened the night before, she might have remained with Edward. It is, ultimately,
Hazel's ignorance of human sexuality that betrays her. Her
dreams of Reddin were the product of instinct, not magic.
Her needs, now awakened but unfulfilled by Edward and untutored by her parents, lead Hazel to Reddin's brutal sexuality. She has no power to resist, since she believes magical
forces rather than human nature determine her actions.

While she sits on a bare hilltop in Hunter's Spinney and
watches the pastoral scene below her, Reddin ascends the hill
from his dark house. His intentions are vague:

He did not confess even to himself why he had come. His thoughts on sex were so prurient that . . . he considered any frankness about it most indecent. Sex was to him a thing that made the ears red. It is hard for them that have breeding stables to enter the kingdom of heaven.[48]

When Hazel and Reddin meet she asks him why he wanted to see her, and he replies that it is for the usual reasons that a man wants to meet a woman. Hazel denies, as she has over and over again, that she is a woman, and as she looks at him she realizes that she does not want him; instead "she wanted freedom and time to find out how much she liked Edward."[49] But it is too late. As Edward Marston is preaching the Sunday evening sermon on the power of prayer to protect the beloved from all harm, Reddin catches Hazel as she runs from him, throws her to the ground and rapes her. Though she feels crushed and robbed, Hazel also feels that she now belongs to Reddin, even though spiritually she remains Edward's. Hazel's Eden of innocence has ended; she and Reddin sense that they have been "trapped by something vast and intangible" and sit in the darkening wood, cowering as if "beneath a hand raised to strike."[50] In a new and terrible passivity, Hazel allows Reddin to put her on his horse. She decides to leave Foxy with Edward, where the little animal is safe, and where she now wishes that she might be also. Reddin installs her at Undern, but Hazel broods over his assumption that she will remain there for good. She has now learned the most blatant facts of sexuality, but she does not yet connect them with pregnancy and maternity.

Although Reddin sobbed after he raped her, although sex initially brings out the better side of his nature and for a short while tenderness seems nearly possible, the best in Reddin is so poorly developed that it is obvious he cannot really change. Edward is all spirit and emotion, unable to acknowledge the body's needs, even when those needs are coupled with love and concern; Reddin is merely body, unredeemed by spiritual love. Neither man is himself whole, and neither

man can, therefore, supply Hazel with the total love that she
needs to grow to womanhood, to learn the demands that
nature will make on her—whether she will accept or not.
Hazel's continued passivity with Reddin enables him to return to his old ways. He begins to hunt again, though he had
earlier promised never to, and he piles his bloody trophies on
the kitchen table for Hazel to see. He begins to contemplate
fatherhood:

That, too, would be a good thing. Two possessions are better than
one, and he could well afford children. It never occurred to him to
wonder whether Hazel would like it, or be sorry for the pain in
store for her. He felt very unselfish as he thought, "When she can't
go about, I'll sit with her now and then."[51]

Yet even in the midst of such "tender" considerations, Reddin
takes a hedgehog from his pocket and tortures it until the
animal sets up a long, continuous scream. When Hazel attempts to beat him from the animal, with blows which were
"by no means so negligible as most women's" since her hands
and arms are quite strong, Reddin throws the animal to the
floor where the hound awaits it. When Hazel turns on the
dog and kicks it, Reddin is amused enough by her passion to
drive the animal from its prey.[52] In Reddin, paternity and
venery go hand in hand.

  Thinking she is with her father, Edward finally learns that
his wife is at Undern. Edward goes there, and he and Reddin
fight, but Edward, in his ministerial softness, is completely
defenseless and Reddin hits him over and over again. Hazel
runs to the fallen Edward, revives him, and, to Reddin's complete surprise, leaves with the loser. Edward's single emotion
at finding Hazel at Undern is relief. He is overjoyed to have
her home again, and his protective instincts, mixed with his
sense of Hazel's innocence, lead him to believe that she has
been held prisoner. Edward thinks that his wife has gone
through the entire experience untouched and unchanged.
Mrs. Marston, however, is less naive: "You will send her
away from here, of course?" is her first comment.[53] The two
women keep wary company of one another for the next six

weeks. Hazel has begun to feel the first symptoms of her pregnancy, but she is ignorant of their meaning. Informed that Sally Haggard has again taken up with Reddin, Hazel is jealous. When Reddin rides by the house one day, Hazel cannot help herself and returns to Undern. Reddin is neither surprised nor grateful; he is triumphant.

Reddin is no less brutal than before; Hazel's pregnancy makes her quieter, which pleases him. He alternates between killing animals—sometimes before Hazel's very eyes—and abusing her. After watching a particularly sadistic killing, Hazel makes it clear that she finds babies ugly; she would prefer to mother animals. Hazel still believes she has such a choice. It is Sally Haggard who informs Hazel of her pregnancy. Hazel is both amazed and terrified. Reddin had done his best to prevent the two women from meeting, but Sally, hoping to convince Hazel that she should leave Reddin, decides to confront Hazel with the children she has had by Reddin. Sally quickly perceives Hazel's pregnancy and her obvious ignorance, and is moved to tell her the truth. Hazel, in turn, is shocked by Reddin's treatment of the woman who has borne his children. When Reddin comes in and sees Sally and raises his arm to strike her, Hazel protects her.

★ ★ ★

This sudden friendship between the two women is brief, both chronologically—it lasts for a few hours on a single day—and in terms of the novel's primary concerns. But it is of some interest since this is the single interaction between Hazel and another woman that is characterized by mutual solicitude—by a sharing not only of stories but also of power so that each may have protection against a mutual threat. Sally Haggard provides Hazel with the knowledge of her pregnancy, so that she can leave Reddin before her fate is similar to her own; Hazel saves Sally from a sure beating. In her genuine concern for Hazel, and in her role as sexual adviser, Sally fulfills the role of surrogate mother. This is the single instance in the entire novel when Hazel finds help from another woman. Yet even this "mother" fails Hazel, for as well-meant as Sally's advice is, her description of pregnancy and birth is so lurid that it leaves Hazel terrified, and her rough attempt to comfort the now shivering Hazel by suggesting that she will find pleasure in producing a fine baby boy, like his father, leaves Hazel in near hysteria for she has no desire to replicate Jack Reddin. She states expressly that it is Edward Marston she would rather have her child resemble.

This momentary mother-daughter relationship between Sally and Hazel has provided Hazel with some of those things mothers traditionally have given their daughters: comfort, concern, sexual knowledge, protection. But it has also provided Hazel with the darker elements of the mother-daughter relationship—that terrible conversation wherein the daughter, newly initiated into maternity, is told of the pain-filled nature of her coming confinement. What the mother offers the daughter as the conventional anodyne for the pain of birth is the production of a male child who resembles the father. But for a daughter who, despite her sexual activity, has rejected maternity, the resemblance of her child to the man she hates is no comfort whatsoever. Hazel, although without a mother except briefly, has never ceased being a daughter. She does not want to be a mother; she did not want to be a wife; and although she has at times enjoyed their sexual passion, she does not want to be Reddin's lover. Maray Woodus, by word and life, demonstrated to Hazel the horrors of marriage. Mrs. Marston, with her adoration of material domesticity and her expectations that Hazel would become the docile servant of all within the house, demanded the loss of that freedom which Hazel finds most intolerable. And Sally Haggard, with her lurid description of pregnancy and birth and with her own bastard brood dressed in rags and thin from hunger, gives verbal and living proof of the validity of Maray Woodus's warning. Hazel has no reason to believe that wifehood and maternity can be pleasurable; nor can she continue to take pleasure in nature since it has betrayed her by a pregnancy that now makes her the object of Reddin's need to possess, rend, and destroy. Hazel has lost everything—freedom, love, trust in nature. And this loss, Webb states, is the stuff of tragedy:

That a woman should, in the evolution of life, cease to be a virgin and become a mother is a thing so natural and so purely physical as hardly to need comment; but that the immortal part of her should be robbed, that she should cease to be part of an entity in a world where personality is the only rare and precious thing—this is tragic.[54]

Like a wounded animal seeking shelter, Hazel finally returns to Edward and the Marston cottage. But Mrs. Marston will have nothing to do with Hazel and scorns her as an adultress. Edward himself, momentarily made cruel by his realization that Hazel was not the pure angel he had foolishly believed, now demands of Hazel the marital rights he had previously abrogated: "I'm not particular. You're not new, but you'll do."[55] For Hazel, Edward's attitude is the last blow. She had expected love from him; instead she realizes that for Edward sex is connected with duties and rights. Edward does finally renounce his mother; he will not allow *her* to denounce his wife, but *he* continues to berate Hazel himself for her sexual unfaithfulness. He announces that he will have both his pleasure and his children from her, and will only forgive her when she gives him a son. Only Hazel's acceptance and willingness to be the mother of his children will enable their marriage to be healed. If she is to have Edward's love and protection, she will have to accept the maternal role she has previously shunned; her protection is dependent on her submission. Edward is a kinder man than brutal Reddin, but his demand is the same: Hazel's value will be determined by her production of a paternal facsimile. When Edward has been reproduced, all will be forgiven. Hazel's sexuality makes her into an object for Marston, an object that, once possessed by another, is now rendered "used" and secondhand. She can be his only when his sexual use of her results in a product—a son—he can call his own.

Edward learns something from his pain. Sending his mother away, he also relinquishes his childish belief in a God of powerful beneficence. He realizes that religion's moral precepts and society's judgments cannot adequately deal with the complexities of human experience. While his love for Hazel is shaped by what he perceives to be the wrongs she has committed, he has the glimmerings of a knowledge that love has little to do with the pious, text-ridden verities he has learned from his church and his mother:

He could no longer believe in a God, or how could such things be? Manhood was denied him. The last torture was not denied him—namely, that he saw the full satire of his position, saw that it was his own love that had destroyed them both. Out of his complete ruin he arose joyless, hopeless, but great in a tenderness so vast and selfless that it almost took the place of what he had lost.[56]

Without his mother and without his faith, Edward finally begins to grow. He makes plans for Hazel and him to live together in some new place. When the congregation sends its elders to warn him to send Hazel away as the only proper act of a Christian man, Edward displays righteous anger. He knows that Hazel loves him now and that she will learn to love him better. He knows that his love for her will be their protection against the world of hypocrites. His previous conventional piety cannot serve the love he has begun to dimly understand.

★   ★   ★

As with *King Lear,* we are led to the novel's last pages hoping that despite the foreshadowing, the prophetic portraits, the bloodstained dress—that all will nonetheless work out and that love will be triumphant amid the cruelty. But the tragedy hinted is at last enacted. Having learned to love through initial loss, Edward will now lose that love, permanently. And having come to accept her inevitable maturity, having learned to love and unite with the human rather than with helpless animals, Hazel must die. And, ironically, Edward will play a part in Hazel's death. Because he does not wish his wife to hear the terrible things being said about her by the elders, he sends her into the woods where he plans soon to join her. They will leave together. In the woods, Hazel hears the clamor of the hunting hounds and realizes that she had not penned up Foxy that day. Hazel runs toward the sounds of the hunt, as both Reddin and Edward, having heard Hazel's screams, try to prevent what they know is about to occur. In her imagination, Hazel sees her fox held in the hands of a huntsman, high above the pack, sees the knife descend and cut the animal in two, and watches it flung to the pack and torn apart. When Foxy, unharmed, comes trotting out of the woods, Hazel picks her up and begins running from the dogs, but she is so heavy with pregnancy that she is impeded. The dogs scent their prey and give chase. "For one instant the hunter and the righteous man, Reddin the destroyer, and Edward the Saviour, saw her sway, small and dark, before the staring sky. Then, as the pack, with a ferocity of triumph, was flinging itself upon her, she was gone."[57]

With her death a terrible cry echoes through the woods, a voice filled with unutterable horror: "Gone to Earth! Gone to Earth!"[58]

* * *

Society's demands, as dictated by the Mrs. Marstons of the world, involve the victimization of the wife by her domestic duties. The demands of childbirth are enormous; the demands of marriage upon a wife, terrible: "A woman must have an amazing genius if she is still a poet after childbirth."[59] For more than the most common of lives to be lived amid the domestic scene takes genius. The life of poet and mother are not mutual, are not simultaneously possible. But in *Gone to Earth,* even when one escapes the social world of village and presbytery, the life of freedom and independence and non-maturity is not possible. Hazel is not, in other words, simply caught within the mesh of society's demands upon its women. She is also caught in a far more terrible trap—one from which she cannot be sprung. Nature—amoral and all-directing natural law—makes its own demands and those cannot be avoided, since to be female is to be body as well as spirit, instinct as well as conscious desire. This notion of the human being as merely another part of the budding, larvae-filled, mating, and gravid world is apparent even in Webb's early poems, where it is a constant theme. But she refuses to see the human female's physicality as having different social meaning from the male's. For Webb, male and female anatomy is equally destined.

★ ★ ★

Throughout the novel, Hazel has been positioned within the landscape or within a room or window or door, and held there for a time, utterly still. Webb's descriptions of these scenes are examples of what her critics found most admirable in her work: the lyrical presentation of landscape. But as skillfully descriptive as these passages are, their purpose is not the presentation of Shropshire's environs. In all of these scenes there lurks an unseen presence. Often this presence is Reddin, who spies upon Hazel from every turn. But just as often, the unseen presence is the watching universe itself. Webb sometimes particularizes the universe as heaven or sky, sometimes as air. But whatever designation she may give it, it is a powerful agent, "vast, solitary, and silent"[60] and perfectly indifferent:

Men only stammer of it in such words as Eternity, Fate, God. All the outcries of all creatures, living and dying, sink in its depths as in an unsounded ocean. Whether this listening silence, incurious, yet hearing all, is benignant or malevolent, who can say? The wistful dreams of men haunt this theme for ever; the creeds of men are so many keys that do not fit the lock. We ponder it in our hearts, and some find peace, and some find terror. The silence presses upon us ever more heavily until death comes with his cajoling voice and promises us the key. Then we run after him into the stillness, and are heard no more.[61]

Hazel's trap was biological—but not nature's demand for reproduction, as Webb believes, but rather the maturing female body's sexual desire. That sexuality *is* her vulnerability because it makes her an object to be possessed, because it can result in pregnancy, against her will and without her understanding of the process, and because maternity's only safety lies in the protection of marriage that demands as payment for that protection the loss of her autonomy. Lacking maternal or paternal figures able to teach her either to accept this construction of the world or a means by which she might avoid total entrapment in such a construction, and lacking either lover or husband able to unite sexual passion and tenderness, Hazel can neither live nor escape. Webb can only have her die, killed by the hunting pack—nature's innocent beasts perverted by human training to run down the fox, a member of the dogs' own family.

The House in Dormer Forest

The Daughter's Love, The Mother's Power

Centuries of custom, centuries of precedent! They pressed,
they crushed, they suffocated. If you gave in to them you
might venture to hope to live somehow, but if you opposed
them you broke yourself to pieces against their iron flanks.
She saw it all; it was not her fault, it was not her mother's fault. They were just two poor straws being asked to
swim against the current of that monster tyrant: "the usual
thing"!

RADCLYFFE HALL, *The Unlit Lamp*

The years between 1917 and 1920 were among the most
tranquil in Webb's life. With Henry's appointment to the
Priory School at Shrewsbury, the Webbs began to build a
small house, Spring Cottage, Lyth Hill; Mary's sense of security was restored. She was now free from close proximity
to her mother, and she finally had a place of her own in which
to write. Webb found herself in the enviable position of being
competed for by several publishers, all of whom were anxious for first rights to her next, and still unwritten, novel. By
autumn 1917, Webb's first two novels had been published in
the United States as well as in England. In October 1917, a
third book appeared as well, *The Spring of Joy,* a collection of
poems and essays, some written during her own first illness
and others written during the long illness following her father's death. Although none of the books sold the thousands
of copies she had wished, she felt secure in her growing readership. She had attained some popularity in the United States,
where her novels had gained her praise for her fusion of realism and romanticism and where her name was already
being linked with that of Thomas Hardy. Three American

firms—Dutton, Doubleday, and George H. Doran—were bidding for her future work. Her advance for her still unwritten third novel was larger than the sum usually paid young authors well before publication; Doran ultimately secured *The House in Dormer Forest* for publication and advanced £300 on future royalties and agreed on a further £300 for its successor, sums that enabled Webb to buy gifts and pay off debts. In addition, she could count in her readership certain well-known critics—Rebecca West, John Buchan, Robert Lynd, and the publisher Sir Ernest Hodder Williams—who saw the promise her work indicated.[1] Even if the plot and structure of *The Golden Arrow* might not be as tight as one would wish, her deftness and humor with characters was attractive, and the passionate force of *Gone to Earth* with its denunciation of hypocritical piety and cold-hearted domesticity hinted of still darker visions to come.

But to say that Webb was happy at Lyth Hill is not to say that she settled into middle-class domestic bliss, nor even that she lived the life of the typical British cottager. It took no time at all for Webb to gain a reputation for eccentricity among her neighbors, although, as Dorothy Wrenn makes clear, Webb was hardly distressed by such a label. She was happy and so she was also healthy again; like the true eccentric, she did as she pleased rather than as her neighbors thought she ought, and either did not notice or did not care that her behavior might be construed as in any way unusual. She was not only highly forgetful—going to town, for instance, with her dress only half-buttoned—but she paid even less attention than usual to the mundane chores of housekeeping. Mending, cleaning, and even cooking were left undone, while Henry often walked about with large holes in his socks. Webb had no qualms about muddying herself by walking through the field even when a perfectly good path ran along the field's edge. Her working habits were erratic in her orderly neighbors' eyes. Her windows would be lit late at night and her curtains still drawn in the morning—evidence that she worked half the night and then slept till well past noon. Other times she would rise at dawn to go berry picking. She would give to anyone she happened to meet along the road the basket of berries or mushrooms she and Henry had just spent an entire morning picking, a generosity the Webbs could ill afford and which their frugal neighbors would hardly appreciate or understand.

As if these peculiarities of behavior were not enough, there was Webb's fascination with the town children.[2] Dorothy Wrenn and Gladys Coles stress that Webb's care of her younger brothers and sisters had developed in her an early and ardent love of children.[3] They seem certain that Webb suffered from her childless state. This may well be true. But Webb's intense fascination with children was doubtless also a product of her own self-absorption. She found in children a reflection of that still immature part of her own psyche, which she cherished—cherished with a love that sometimes produced creative energy but more often resulted in terrible self-pity. She responded to children less as a mother longing to fulfill her role, than as a child longing to join her playmates. She developed the habit of spying upon a family who regularly picnicked nearby. As the family ate, Webb would hide behind her garden hedge and peer at them silently. The children, in turn, would not speak to Mary, having been warned by their parents that she was "a bit queer."[4]

Along with this silent watching from the hedges, Webb took a great pleasure in surprising children in the neighborhood with gifts: a bicycle, a piano, clothing. That such gifts were well beyond the means of Henry's salary, and that her choices were not always practical or even usable—she sent a six-year-old child tiny kid booties—did not seem to interfere with her pleasure.[5] Her biographers are most interesting in their treatment of this aspect of Webb's life. They praise her generosity and view her behavior as evidence of a saintly way of life. Even as levelheaded a critic as Wrenn descends to rustic-saint rhetoric when describing Webb's activities behind the garden privet as she watched the children picnicking: "She would steal to the hedge at the side of her garden and watch them, like a little brown bat with great brooding eyes";[6] or, "She did not mind that the picnic party did not speak to her;

to watch them was enough and more than enough."[7] Wrenn suggests that Webb had become a watcher of children rather than active in their games because she feared that her marred appearance—her protuberant eyes and goiter—would frighten the children.[8] While this is a possibility, descriptions of those who knew her during this period include no mention of physical deformity but rather describe her as small, slim, and strikingly attractive.[9]

What explains Webb's inappropriate generosity or her apparent lack of concern for Henry's needs? It is not simply that Henry's socks went without mending, a minor matter he himself might attend to even though the Webbs' neighbors would certainly assume it was his wife's responsibility to darn. Webb's brother suggests that Henry was quite willing to put up with dirty dishes and odd meals, because he recognized that his wife's happiness lay in her writing.[10] Wrenn admits, however, to some qualms at Henry's situation in light of his wife's financial impracticality.[11] During this period, Webb identified intensely with the weak and suffering, and ignored what seemed to her to be life's more mundane matters. The practical needs of the recipients of her gifts were secondary to the psychic need that her generosity satisfied. The financial strain caused by her gift-giving was eclipsed by her pleasure in giving another what she herself desired. Webb gave what she would have. She satisfied the child in herself far more than she satisfied the children of Lyth Hill. This is especially true if Gladys Coles is correct in stating that many of the gifts Webb gave were torn up or given away in anger because they were so unsuitable.[12] The six-year-old who received those kid booties remained a baby in Webb's memory; she was not interested in his growth but in what he symbolized in herself. The children of a family who all received the exact same hat in the same exact size—although they were of three quite different ages—were not considered individuals but replicas; they were the interchangeable projections of herself as child.[13]

If this was a tranquil time for Webb, perhaps it was so not simply because she had returned to her beloved Shropshire and to Lyth Hill, but also because she was able to spend these years as mother to her own child self. Although she never bore a child, Webb was nonetheless both parent and off-spring, able to supply, at least symbolically, what she had craved. It would be gratifying if such self-nurturing resulted in self-healing. But it did not. Immediately after this brief three-year hiatus, Webb became ill again. Coles suggests that this illness was aggravated by the cool reception given *The House in Dormer Forest*.[14] Wrenn states that Mary's doctor blamed her illness on her solitude and melancholic brood-ing.[15] Webb had also begun to argue with her mother again.[16] Any one of these factors could have caused the symptoms of Graves' disease to recur. But Webb's creeping about, the im-moderate nature of her Lady Bountiful activities, her strange behavior, signify that her self-mothering did not heal an old psychic wound either, did not integrate childhood's needs with adulthood's power. The child was being indulged but the adult remained unsatisfied. In a letter written to a friend during this period, Webb wrote that she now possessed "the lovely impossible things that I long for . . . to live on Lyth Hill, and to live in a house of my own."[17] But there were other "lovely impossible things" that were not to be had, things never consciously recognized which marred both her life and work, causing the former to be filled with depression and fear and the latter to be flawed by inconsistency, as in the case of *The House in Dormer Forest*.

★ ★ ★

In her first two novels Webb enables daughters to become selves separate from their mothers by creating a distance, emotional or physical, between them. Webb banished one mother to the kitchen and buried another. In *The House in Dormer Forest* Webb creates a mother so cruel in her domestic tyranny that there is no danger of the good daughter seeking to emulate her. The daughter's separation—her identity—is achieved because the daughter is made "better"—kinder, more sensitive, more honest—than her mother. Distance is achieved through virtue.

Susan Peck MacDonald suggests that even the good, sup-
portive mother is a questionable blessing for those daughters
who choose to emulate her role.[18] And for those daughters
who forsake that maternal role, she is a threat, a living re-
minder of their failure to meet her expectations. The influ-
ential mother who is also highly critical—a mother such as
Alice Meredith—is a double threat for such a daughter. If the
daughter seeks to discredit her mother's influence, the mother's evaluations must be shown to be flawed. In turn, the
daughter's worthiness must be made clear. *The House in Dormer Forest* attempts to perform this restructuring of worthiness: mothers and the daughters who emulate them are
shown to be wrong, if not actually evil. The daughter who
evades imitation of her mother is shown to be best: she is
rewarded with a husband who loves her and the promise of
true, if probably childless, happiness.

★　★　★

Like Undern Hall of *Gone to Earth,* Dormer House is an
amalgamation of all the lives lived within it, past and present.
Its architecture is a mixture of various styles: Elizabethan,
Queen Anne, Georgian, Grecian. At its center, however, is
the original house, an ancient English cottage "which seemed
to be the nucleus of the whole . . . neglected now . . . and
weighed down by the large-leafed ivy, haunted by its whisper
year after year."[19] Unlike Undern, however, Dormer has no
potential for life and redemption: "The house, as a whole,
had something of a malignant air, as of an old ruler from
whom senility takes the power, but not the will, for tyranny.[20] While nature has the power to obliterate the house,
shrouding it in heavy mists that linger in the area "as of in-
alienable right," and while the wild landscape is ruled by the
"white owls and the hasty water and the mazy bat-dances,"[21]
those within Dormer know that they are enmeshed in a web
of social rules and customs "so complex as to render the individual soul almost helpless."[22] Dormer House is both symbol and matrix for the social conventions by which all, but
especially women, must live their lives:

It is the mass-ego that constructs dogmas and law; for while the individual soul is, if free at all, self-poised, the mass-mind is always uncertain, driven by vague, wandering aims; conscious, in a dim fashion, of its own weakness, it builds round itself a grotesque structure in the everlastingness of which it implicitly believes. When each unit of humanity merges itself in the mass, it loses its bearings and must rely on externals. The whole effort of evolution is to the development of individual souls who will dare to be free of the architecture of crowd-morality. For when man is herded, he remembers the savage.[23]

A forest surrounds Dormer House. Various inhabitants had, through successive generations, attempted to fell the trees, but had been daunted by the magnitude of the task. Those trees, regenerating even as the house dies, look down on Dormer "like people looking at something grotesque, not with blame or praise, but in a disdainful kind of indifference."[24] Nature plays no part in Dormer's human rituals. Those who would escape the confines of social rite and expectation must "prefer the dour laws of earth to the drag of the herd of man-kind, and fly from the house of man to the forest, where the emotionless silence always seems to be gathering, as waves mount and swell, to the disclosure of a mystery."[25] This indifference of nature does not hamper development of the individual. The interference of society rather than the awesome amorality of the forest warps the human spirit.

Human interference and stifling ritual characterize life at Dormer House. The present inhabitants are the Darke family, consisting of Solomon and Rachel Darke, Rachel's mother, Grandmother Velindre, the four Darke children, Amber, Ruby, Jasper, and Peter, as well as Catherine Velindre, a distant relative who lives there as a paying guest. The five women of the Darke family span three generations and offer contrasting portraits of women seeking power. Rachel Darke is in her prime; she rules the house and those who dwell within it through a carefully and cruelly manipulative silence. Grandmother Velindre, once the powerful matriarch, is now dominated by her own daughter, Rachel, who allows her mother virtually no freedom, just as her mother once denied her any autonomy. Catherine Velindre, who first decides to marry Peter, then Jasper, and finally Michael Hallowes, hopes through marriage to gain power over Dormer and over Rachel, thus continuing the matriarchal rule begun with Grandmother Velindre. Ruby seeks the freedom, independence, and social status she believes marriage will confer. Amber alone is aware of the power struggle that goes on within the house, and Amber alone seeks escape from Dormer's rule rather than a continuance of it. At the novel's conclusion, it is Amber, aging and unattractive, who has found and married a man who loves her.

Despite the fact that this novel details the complexity of maternal domination, none of the novel's critics have focused on this particular aspect. The mother-daughter relationship is completely ignored, even by recent critics, and even by those who examine the novel at some length. Because the novel's major focus has been ignored, there is no agreement among the critics about its meaning. Thomas Moult and Glen Cavaliero say that *The House in Dormer Forest* is concerned with the effects of civilization and social ritual on the creative spirit.[26] Wrenn judges the novel a comedy, filled with a gentle perception of people and their foibles.[27] Coles discusses the novel in terms of its development of Webb's mystic philosophy,[28] and suggests that this novel is Webb's most significant.[29] Wrenn and Cavaliero are at odds in their critical estimation of the novel, Cavaliero finding the characters wooden and manipulated, while Wrenn believes that this is the first novel in which Webb created characters who exist in their own right and act from a believably established personality.[30] Although she considers the novel highly reflective of Webb's own spiritual development, Wrenn denies that the novel has any significant autobiographical aspect. She believes *The House in Dormer Forest* is a novel of a woman finally personally secure enough to write without projecting her own unhappy psyche.[31]

Not one of these critics considers *The House in Dormer Forest* a novel in which Webb attempts to grapple with her complex relationship to her own mother, and a novel in which she considers that relationship in terms of personal biography and in the larger terms of women's domestic lives. Wrenn and Coles do both note that the novel makes telling statements about the spiritual maternity of women who love but have no children of their own. They relate such statements to Webb's unhappiness with her childless state during this period. But such statements can be seen as reflecting the needs of a child-less author-daughter who seeks a rejoinder to her multiparous mother's expectations, and seeks a positive response from her even as she rejects the mother's power to demand such a response from her daughter.

And because these critical readings have downplayed the importance of the mother-daughter power struggle, they have also noted as of minor significance one of the most prominent features of its landscape, the grotto, and the topiary avenue of yew trees that leads to it, the Beast Walk. Coles seems correct in her suggestion that the Beast Walk symbolizes the collective and personal unconscious mind filled with instinctual drives, desires, and repression.[32] However, because she sees *The House in Dormer Forest* as representative of Webb's mystical development, she examines the grotto and Beast Walk in terms of their biblical allegorical significance, not as related to maternal power, as they seem to be.

The topography of the grotto and the Beast Walk suggest a nightmare landscape where shapes from the past still live but now made strange and deformed by time, waiting to prey upon the dreamer. The origin of the dream's topography is both personal and collective; it is determined by individual psychic history but emerges, as well, from the collective unconscious of the species. Its sources, in other words, are simultaneously clear and murky. Just as the matrix of the dream can be traced, but not by logical paths, so too, the Beast Walk emerges from lightless water: "There was something significant in the way in which this broad and rather pompous walk ended in the soft, thick stream without reason or explanation.[33] The walk is so old that even Grandmother

Velindre can only recall being told by *her* grandmother that it had been completed during her own "archaic childhood."[34] The Walk's history is nearly forgotten, but what little is known is passed down by the women—by the matriarchs of the Darke family. Over the centuries, each generation of the family had cut one or two shapes into the yew trees—those trees most often found in cemetery landscapes—but no gardener's art had been precise. As the generations passed, the figures became nearly indistinguishable: "all had a nightmare touch."[35] Beaks and claws had grown to exaggerated proportions; the shapes of "head and wing and udder became vague and ominous. They were a herd of prehistoric beasts trooping down to drink at the stream."[36] For Jasper, drawn to the Beast Walk when feeling misunderstood because he cannot conform to his family's expectations, the place symbolizes all the ancient traditions and "predatory collectivism" of Dormer House. He is as much repelled as fascinated by the place. In the evening, when the sky is threatening a storm, the beasts of the Walk are tinged red by the sky's lurid colors. At the end of the Walk, built of flat gray stones, is the grotto which in the odd light appears almost like a waiting sacrificial altar.[37]

The Walk and grotto suggest an ancient age of social tradition, and that tradition's demand for the sacrifice of individual desire. Like Dormer House itself, both the Beast Walk and the grotto are the creation of the familial past and have embodied the twisted shapes of that repressive history. Just as the Beast Walk is remembered by the matriarchs of the Darke family, so the grotto is a creation of the Darke women.[38] These "staid ladies" did not know why they built this place so patiently, why they lined it with the pale mother-of-pearl shells. It had been built for the "tame revellings of conventional ladyhood, and behold! that rough, wild thing, young passion, took possession."[39] It is in the grotto that Peter seduces Marigold, the servant girl whom he finally secretly marries. And it is in the grotto that Enoch, the simple, mystical shepherd who also loves Marigold, fights his temptation to murder Peter. In the grotto Catherine tests Jasper's love by demanding that he forsake his decision to leave the ministry. And it is here that Michael Hallowes spurns Catherine's advances because he loves Amber. The grotto becomes the site of love perverted by lust, power, and violence, perverted precisely because love's innocent eroticism and intense spirituality are denied in the interests of social ritual and material power, jealousy, and gross sensuality.

But while the Beast Walk and grotto serve as metaphor for the novel's concern with the strangling effect of tradition on individual growth, they function as metaphor, as well, for the dark horrors that result when female sexuality is twisted to meet the demands of conventional marriage and maternity. The dark path that leads from marshy banks to the mother-of-pearl, pink-lined grotto suggests a vulval topography.[40] The Beast Walk exerts a "dark spell" over Jasper, who drinks there of a "charm thick as black honey made from purple poison flowers by bees in hell."[41] Fearsome though the Walk is, Jasper is compelled to enter it; its force is irresistible. Deep within the grotto, the pearly chamber glows in the light of the lovers' candles, glows in shades of "saffron, salmon pink, of veined purple and scarlet."[42] Within its shell-lined chambers, Peter and Marigold make illicit love, Peter like some wood-god and Marigold a forbidden fruit about to be despoiled.[43] Peter does not love Marigold, though he is certainly embroiled in a youthful eroticism that passes for love. He is, as well, infatuated with Marigold's beauty. And he is aware that he can use her love for him to seduce her. He has no intention of marrying the servant girl; Peter, unlike Jasper, has always conformed to Dormer's expectations. And besides, Peter intends to marry Catherine; he is completely unaware that Catherine has already decided that Jasper, if he will only recant his theological foolishness, is the better marriage choice. Catherine is sure that Jasper will someday make a fine bishop—and she the perfect bishop's wife.

★   ★   ★

It is the female landscape of the Beast Walk and grotto which is Dormer's heart, and within its vulval geography occur all the cruel, brutal, and lust-filled actions that sex unredeemed by love can cause. Thus at the novel's metaphorical center is the sexual, female body to which the Darke children are drawn. It is a body whose shadowed and cruelly shaped external manifestation is both fascinating and fear-inspiring, and whose womblike interior provides a place for the distortions of human sexuality. The Walk and the grotto, created by men of the ancient past and decorated by archaic women, resemble the construction of the family: fashioned by men but maintained by women. Webb sees the terrible underpinnings of the domestic sphere as not merely dependent on the presence of a woman—the "Angel of the House" so honored by the Victorians—but as founded on men's conflicting need and fear of the vagina. Webb sees the ways in which history has tried to shape and change women to its own ends. And she understands the family as the locus, not of love and protection, but of all love's perversions and cruelties. What Webb refuses to see is that it is not the mother who has made the family what it is.

Undern Hall of *Gone to Earth* had the potential for redemption; sleeping rather than dead, Undern could have become a place of life and its dark history could have been overcome if Reddin had been able to love Hazel. The Marsden cottage, a museum of propriety, also could have become a refuge from the overpowering natural world that surrounded it if Mrs. ing natural world that surrounded it if Mrs. Marsden had been capable of love rather than hypocritical piety, or if Edward had been able to unite his immense spiritual love with physical passion, or if Hazel had been able to overcome her daughter's innocence. The Devil's Chair cottage, which the newlyweds build in *The Golden Arrow,* is filled with love and comfort, despite its ominous location, because Deborah and Stephen learn there the beginnings of the mutual self-sacrifice love demands. Once, however, that bond of selflessness is destroyed by Stephen's abandonment, Deborah finds the cottage frightening and oppressive, and she ultimately burns it and all its contents to the ground. Houses without love, in other words, are not neutral but threaten death. They must be abandoned and destroyed, or they will kill.

At the conclusion of *The House in Dormer Forest,* Grandmother Velindre sets fire to the house, her decision based on her thoroughly dotty interpretation of a biblical text. However, although the house burns to the ground, the Beast Walk and grotto remain intact. Grandmother dies while watching the fire she has set; Rachel Darke stands stunned at the sight of what she is losing: "She wanted the old vampire dwelling."[44] But the several pairs of lovers, variously happy, have already left Dormer. The power of Dormer House itself is destroyed; Grandmother is dead; Rachel Darke cannot rule without the tradition and ritual that the house provided; the lovers are distant and therefore safe. But the ever remaining forest, cold and uncaring of the fate of humans and their creations, contemplates the conflagration. Seemingly aflame, the Beast Walk's topiaries turn scarlet in the reflected glow of Dormer's fire. In fact, they are spared by the fire, which destroys the more obvious symbol of human tradition and social ritual. But the fire cannot, it would seem, destroy the primeval source of human desire—the maternal body. While the fearful power of Rachel Darke and Grandmother Velindre is ended, the ancient matrix of the Darke family's maternal power remains whole and untouched at the center of Dormer's remains. Individual daughters, such as Amber, may flee the past to seek their own present and create their own future, but the threat of the maternal body nonetheless remains.

These suggestions of a threatening maternal body seem unrelievedly Freudian, while the hint of a collective unconscious filled with maternal archetypes is certainly Jungian. Though both psychoanalytic and Jungian approaches to Webb's literature can offer insights into the seeming opacity of the romantic tale of this novel and the others, both approaches reduce the complexity of the works since, strictly applied, both Freudian and Jungian interpretations posit as the normal and healthy standard the patriarchal structuring of culture, family, and female development. In this, as in her subsequent novels, Webb is searching for a means by which the female body with its sexuality, its intellectual vigor and drive, its demands for love, freedom, and power can both love and remain individual. She seeks a means by which the powerful mother can be destroyed, a means by which her hold on her life and identity can be lessened, and a lover found, while the daughter yet lives guilt-free and whole.

Webb's fascination with the village (and later, London) children, her attempt to shower them with gifts of inappropriate nature and magnitude, her preoccupation with proving that childless women were as capable of maternal feelings as biological mothers—all suggest that Webb in her personal life attempted to become her mother via surrogate maternity, and become, as well, her own child/daughter through her identification with the neighborhood children. It seems clear that she attempted to be the bountiful, generous, whimsical mother her own had not. To become her mother—but better than her mother—is one method of destroying the powerful but bad mother. Webb's obsession with children is an attempt to find some way to negate the "wrong" mother and in her place substitute the good daughter who is also her own mother and so deny the "wrong" mother's power. The attempt is successful in Webb's novels. By the conclusion of her writing career, Webb finds a way to live with maternal figures, but only when they are not powerful. The attempt does not succeed as well in real life where, alive or dead, the mother yet remains, just outside the boundaries of fantasy and its enactment.

The House in Dormer Forest successfully annihilates maternal power and its strictures. Those daughters who would continue the maternal power structure by emulating their mothers are shown to be vain and stupid at the very best; at the worst, such daughters are morally corrupt. Only the daughter who refuses to emulate her mother's role is good. The five women of the Darke family span three generations. While in *The Golden Arrow* and *Gone to Earth* mothers are either banished or absent, here they are multiplied. And no daughter loves her mother, no mother her daughter. Grandmother Velindre dominates all at Dormer except Rachel Darke, her own daughter who now has the power over her mother which once her mother exerted over her. At the grandmother's least infraction of Rachel's notion of what is proper—too large a bow on her cap, for instance—Rachel threatens her with being locked up. Silent, icy, and cruel, Rachel Darke is Dormer's ruler, although she is content to disguise her power, letting others think that it is the grandmother who remains matriarch:

Mrs. Darke said nothing but her spirit seemed to weigh on them all like an iceberg silently pressing upon a ship. Her silence was alarming. The less she said, the more she seemed to say. Sometimes it seemed as if she were a ventriloquist, and talked through her mother. [45]

Catherine Velindre is highly aware of the complicated game of puppet-mastery between mother and daughter. On more than one occasion Catherine has used that game to her own advantage. It is obvious to all that Catherine intends to succeed to power herself someday, by her marriage to one of the Darke men. But Catherine labors under the delusion that she can rule and yet be free from those things which enslaved the other women of the family.

Ruby, too, will succeed to the matriarchy, although with far less crafty intelligence than Catherine and with none of Amber's passion. Ruby, full-figured, rosy-cheeked, and materialistic, longs to marry and have her own house in which she is mistress. She succeeds in marrying, but finds herself still caught at Dormer, still under her mother's rule. Because she lacks the ability to be cruel, she is unable to resist the demands and directives of her always proper husband, Ernest. At the novel's conclusion Ernest is offered a post as curate in a distant parish, and Ruby finally will be free to be mistress of her own house. But her obsession with material goods, her new child, and her husband's character make it obvious that Ruby will never be more than a shallow imitation of an individual. She will never have her mother's and grandmother's passion for power; she will never have Catherine's ability to manipulate to her own advantage. Neither will she have Amber's ability to love.

It is Amber alone, of all the Darke women, who loves and who understands the matriarchal structure of the family yet remains free from its power and destruction. Amber is past thirty, unattractive because of her poor complexion, and lightly valued by all her family, even by Jasper, the brother she loves most. But Amber is also a mystic, Webb's first truly developed female example of the type. Deborah Arden, however, was certainly likely to become a mystic; she was, after all, her father's pupil and learned from him to read nature and natural phenomena as an always elusive but always hint-filled script of life's larger meaning, and Hazel Woodus, had she matured, could only have been a mystic since her allegiance was to the larger world of nature rather than the smaller one of human commerce. For Webb, the mystic is the true individual, since it is the mystic who abjures what others would have her be and becomes what she truly is. To become the complete self means, in Webb's metaphysic, to succeed in uniting body and soul. It is the mystic, therefore, who loves best of all for she invests the physical with the spiritual and the spiritual with the sexual, and thus has no need to seek power. The love of the mystic is a "safe" love; her maternal instincts are to comfort and understand rather than to rule and seduce. Amber alone truly escapes Dormer, because she does not bring with her the values and strictures of its world.

*   *   *

With the exception of Amber, the women of this novel are enslaved. Just as Hazel Woodus was enmeshed in the forces of nature which demanded of women that they reproduce, and the forces of society which demanded that maternity entail the sacrifice of personal freedom, so the women of the Darke household are servants to similar forces—patriarchal society's need to continue exactly as it is. Traditions must be maintained and families must carry on from generation to generation. Each woman must do what her mother did, be what she was. Each woman must replicate what went before her, a link in an unvarying chain that must not be broken. In the world of the forest, nature is the amoral force which, regardless of human intent, shapes lives and orders destinies. Human hands can shape the beasts of the Walk only initially; in the end they will take on their own wild forms. In the world of *The House in Dormer Forest,* Webb makes history the amoral shaping force, but she has misnamed the agent. Patriarchy is the shaper of all the lives in this novel, even Rachel's. Rachel may pull Grandmother Velindre's strings, and she may direct the fate of all within her domain, but Darke traditions make Rachel no more than a puppet herself.

Webb does not present these women as prisoners only of history. Each woman is also a prisoner of herself; each is imprisoned by her own inability to love. Like all women, the Darke women have no way out of the cycle. They can choose to love and forsake the dark tradition that waits for them in Dormer's half-lit rooms. Of course, such love will mean, most likely, marriage and possibly children; history is thus ultimately triumphant. But interestingly enough, we do not see maternity as the outcome of Amber's love for Michael Hallowes.

The novel ends on a passionate but childless note. As with Stephen Southernwood in *The Golden Arrow,* Michael Hallowes is indifferently willing to "do the right thing" by Amber, who has spent the night in his cottage. They will marry, although both lovers make it clear that marriage is a silly convention, since their love has already been solemnized and sacramentalized by their souls, which spoke when they first met. In a novel that maintains the stultifying effect of social ritual and religious demand on the human heart, Webb, like Michael Hallowes, does right by Amber. Their love is better, greater, more passionate, more spiritual, truer, and more filled with teasing and tenderness than any other in the vicinity of Dormer forest—if not all England. And each partner is utterly without regard for the social proprieties of ritual and ceremonies; indeed, Michael himself has left the seminary because he does not believe in God. But the socially proper action is performed, just as it was in *The Golden Arrow.* As with domesticity and maternity, Webb can deny the importance of such social rituals as marriage, but she cannot actually reject them. Cohabitation would be as blessed as marriage for Amber and Michael, but Webb has them marry nonetheless.

A third force also holds the Darke women in thrall: the

presumption that each woman will continue the role presented by her mother. Mrs. Darke and Grandmother Velindre are the continual enforcers of their culture's mores. The grandmother's religion is the means whereby she imposes on her grandchildren the behavior proper for their class. Rachel Darke uses her cold silence. Catherine indicates her assent to the continuation of this matriarchal power in her treatment of Jasper; she will withhold her love until he once again accepts Christianity. She does this not because she is interested in the good of Jasper's soul but because she believes that he has the makings of a future high churchman. Even Solomon Darke, the weak and uninterested father whose name belies his wisdom, enforces proper behavior, refusing Jasper pocket money until such time as he again accepts God.

★   ★   ★

Thus a relentless force directs the lives of all the inhabitants of Dormer House—but this is a force that is chosen and a shackle that is freely worn. One can deny society's values; one can love rather than rule: Amber is the proof. All humanity is in servitude to a great and mysterious power that demands the continuation of the species, but Webb maintains that there is room within that demand for the human spirit to grow to its fullest. And for Webb, that spirit is fullest that loves the best.[46] Once again, as in *The Golden Arrow,* Webb looks to universal love as redemptive, as able to deny the horrors of social ritual's stultification of the human spirit; she chooses the word "human" because it ignores the problems particular to women and romantic love.

Webb is distinctly unsympathetic to those Darke women who choose power over passion and love. Nowhere in the novel is there forgiveness for Grandmother Velindre, Rachel Darke, or Catherine. Even Ruby, whose future suffering and whose own selfishness we see in their inception, is depicted as getting only what she deserves. Marrying for dresses and jewelry—she delays the ceremony on her wedding day until she is assured of a dress allowance from her husband—Ruby has shallow needs. Although not a bad woman but rather as kind as her nature allows, Ruby may deserve better than she

will get from Ernest, but she would be incapable of appre-
ciating more than he has to offer. Ernest is all pompous piety
and hearty propriety, hiding greed and lust. Ruby is solely
interested in the importance she will gain as bride and wife,
but Ernest is primarily interested in access to Ruby's body.

Although Webb has no forgiveness even for kind-hearted,
silly Ruby, she has a clear comprehension of the forces that
create such women as Rachel Darke, Catherine, and Grandmother. Having been powerless in their youth, they could not
in adulthood refuse the joy of tyranny: "The desire had
grown into a lust. To tyrannize was metheglin. . . ."[47] The
youthful impotence of these women is the result of their
mother's role as the enforcer of patriarchal values. The
daughter is denied power, even over herself, and refused responsibility for her own actions and decisions. Marriage is
the only escape from such maternal and familial domination,
but, of course, marriage merely starts the process over.
Rachel Darke married not for love but because she hated her
family and could no longer bear to be part of her household.[48]
The result of a marriage entered into for such reasons is not
simply the misery of a loveless relationship with a man whose
very grammar would drive her to distraction, but far worse:
inevitable motherhood. Webb depicts maternity's power over
daughters, and the daughters' exchange of adolescent impotence for wifehood's domain and maternal domination. But
what is obviously missing in this depiction is the patriarch's
rule of domain and his own role as dominator. Webb would
place the blame for the daughter's first unhappiness on the
mother. The adult daughter's unhappiness she views as the
result of the daughter's emulation of her mother. Fathers may
be weak or even foolish, like Solomon Darke, but they are
blameless; they are not the cause of the adult female's unhappiness. Once again Webb places the attainment of happiness
in the hands of the individual woman; she *can* achieve her own
desires if only she will eschew her mother's lessons. As long
as mothers are the cause of the daughters' pain, patriarchy's
role in creating such tyrannical mothers and aspiring-to-

power daughters can be ignored. Women *can* be happy in the patriarchy since it is mothers who are at fault.

★ ★ ★

So unhappy was Mrs. Darke with her own maternity that she refused to name her children. Webb's description of husband and wife, the cradle between them, delineates the terrible anger Rachel Darke's silence both hides and conveys, as well as Solomon's complete ineffectiveness:

> Mrs. Darke had been so bored by the advent of each child . . . that she refused to think of any names for them. There had been many long silent conflicts when her husband sat, moody and obstinate, staring at the mute bundle in the majestic cradle which was a Darke heirloom, and saying at long intervals: "Give it a name, Rachel!"
>
> Mrs. Darke, equally obstinate, on her large sofa with its uncomfortable ornaments of carved mahogany leaves, silently tore calico. The argument, wordless on one side, always ended without a name having been found; and though Solomon's nerves were those of a ploughman, they at last became irritated by the harsh, regular tearing, and by that in his wife's character which lay behind the tearing and caused it.
>
> "What are you making, tearing so?" he would ask angrily. And she would reply, like scissors snapping, "Binders!"[49]

Throughout the novel, Mrs. Darke is to be found tearing fabric, but it is not difficult to see the added significance of her prophetic "Binders!" She will swaddle—immobilize—her children. Her quest for power is not a desire to rule many, but only those few within her family whom she binds to herself through fear, through the enforcement of social proprieties, through religion, through money. "What she wanted was the human soul. On that she fed, on that she gloated as any cannibal might. If it fled from her, she clutched at it; if it escaped she used all her finesse to catch it again, having caught it, she tore it in bitter, silent rage."[50]

The cruelties of Mrs. Darke and of her mother are not innate. They are not two flawed samples of the human spirit, but damaged souls. Strong women who were denied the power to become fully capable, each became warped, using such power as she had to bind and hurt others instead of developing herself. And as mothers, each did to her daughters just as her mother had done to her. History repeats itself, not simply by means of the maternal womb, but by means of maternal vengeance for the wrongs of her own girlhood.

It is interesting that Webb creates no obstacles to Rachel Darke's actions, just as she has Grandmother Velindre dominate her daughter's early life without any interference. Solomon Darke is a weak man, yet he is still capable of acting as *pater familias* when the matter concerns a son: he decides the professions of Jasper and Peter; he can and does punish each. But it would seem that a father does not interfere in the relationship between mother and daughter. Solomon ignores as much as possible what goes on around him. His world is that of hunting dogs, account books, and the evening paper. Not particularly intelligent nor particularly strong, he is a new type of paternal figure not encountered in Webb's two earlier novels. He is a kind man without malice but who, in his need to protect his role as head of the house, perpetrates deeds which cause the more sensitive members spiritual agony. Amber is fondly protective of her father. She is amused by his attempts to solve the puzzles in his weekly paper, and she is always a bit sad at his inevitable failure.

Solomon Darke's ineffectual kindness is tinged by the animal-like aspects of physiognomy. Solomon may resemble the dumb ox, but it is the cruel dog of the hunt that dominates:

The expressionless heaviness of his face was redeemed by something of the patience of oxen, and rendered intimidating by a hint of the bull-dog in the mouth's ferocious tenacity. It was obvious that his one idea in any crisis would be to resort to physical force.[51]

Rachel Darke's covert manipulations are matched by her husband's barely concealed brutality. The mother's malice and the father's violence are the generative forces of Dormer House.

★   ★   ★

The dual nature of female sexuality—that it makes a woman both vulnerable and powerful—is depicted in Ruby and Catherine. Ruby is the victim of her own ripe beauty. She seeks freedom from her mother and indulgences from her husband, but Ernest seeks sex. Ruby has married for the same reasons as her mother did; and continuing that tradition, Ruby resents her maternity. While there is an amusing aspect to Ruby's dislike of her child—he resembles Ernest, certainly reason enough for her displeasure—we see in Ruby a replication of Rachel. That Ruby is the scatterbrain rather than the binding, tearing mother redeems her to an extent; Ruby is hardly her mother's equal in cruelty. Ruby is too petty to be truly evil. In her indolent, full-bodied, slightly blowsy way, Ruby represents a sort of feminine innocence; she attracts Ernest, but she has few wiles. She is certainly not seductive nor does she consciously use the power of her sexuality, as does Catherine, to extort favors or to manipulate. That she wins her dress allowance, that she succeeds in wearing white satin rather than the simple muslin Catherine proposes as far more suitable for her wedding gown, that she is given the ribbons and bows and silks she feels are her due as a bride are the result of Ruby's sulks and tears and tiny tantrums. She manipulates, but as a child might, and for the same bright, foolish things. Sweet and slightly selfish, Ruby will never assume much power over her own life or that of others. She will be content as long as she has dresses of suitable variety and number. Like her father, Ruby will be an indifferent and ineffectual parent, but she will not cause malicious damage. Webb makes it clear that Ruby's indifference is far preferable to Rachel's interference.

While Ruby is feminine beauty barely conscious of its sexual power, Catherine Velindre is her exact opposite. Certainly she is Ruby's physical opposite, a near Pre-Raphaelite portrait: pale, fragile, aristocratic; her hair is intricately bound, her gaze both meditative and seductive, her hands long and white and graceful. Using religion as her medium, Catherine practices to perfect the image of herself as madonna and saint.

In her bedroom she has carefully placed an enormous crucifix so as to throw a most becoming shadow across her face and throat as she kneels to pray—her bedroom door artfully left ajar. In a formal picture taken of her and given to select male friends, she has posed herself with her eyes raised dramatically toward heaven, an attitude calculated to show off her throat and shoulders. Hers is a mixture of devotion and seduction, nearly irresistible to the two Darke sons:

> By one of the ironies of things, Catherine's religious words and looks were acceptable, not because they were real, but because she looked and spoke with the eyes and lips of a courtesan. Not that Catherine was anything but innocent and ignorant; she was virginal to the point of exasperation; but there was something cold in the allure of her eyes, something knife-like in her smile, that recalled the loveless sisterhood.[52]

Catherine uses her beauty and sexuality to gain her ends, attempting to master her world by mastering its men.

Until she discovers his dalliance with Marigold, Catherine had set her designs on Peter, the eldest son. She then transfers her attentions to Jasper, who promptly becomes blindly infatuated; at the same time she continues to flirt with Philip Arkinstall. She has no intentions of marrying Philip, but she can certainly appreciate the effect his attentions have upon Jasper. When she meets Michael Hallowes, Catherine herself is smitten. Michael, on the other hand, prefers Amber and tells Catherine so. He flatly rejects Catherine's overtures when she offers herself to him. Denied by a man for the first time in her life, Catherine finds herself suddenly in the power of Philip Arkinstall, who has observed Catherine meeting Michael and offering herself to him. Timing his moves carefully, Philip takes Catherine into his arms as she is walking alone, tears her dress off her shoulder, loosens her hair, and kisses her passionately at the exact moment a servant passes. Now, he declares, she must marry him since her reputation will otherwise be lost.

Catherine's virginity was her real power. As the men

around her fought to possess her, Catherine planned to rule the winner's house, just as Rachel did Dormer. It is, of course, ironic that the posturing and manipulating religious hypocrisy of Catherine is outdone by Philip's planned posture and quite literal manipulation. He knows that it is reputation and not fact that makes a woman's virginity a powerful bargaining tool. Once she has lost the name of virgin, Catherine is powerless. She marries Philip, the man she never wanted, as Amber marries Michael, the man she did want.

Seen as a group, the women of Dormer House present a portrait of all the ways by which women attain power, direct their lives and those of others, and enter into marriage and maternity. Women marry most often for escape from family and in order to gain the power to rule themselves—or at least choose their own dresses. Very few marry for love. Women dislike their husbands, scorn them, are afraid of them, are used by them and loved by them. Women use religion, sexuality, beauty, propriety, and the power of love in order to get their way. Some women who are mothers dislike their children, and use them for their own ends. Other women who are not mothers—such as Amber—are capable of a selfless maternal love:

For the real mother is, first, a passionate lover of her children, recklessly spending herself in the manner of all lovers. The idea of either Mrs. Velindre or her daughter in the guise of a reckless lover had in it more of mirth than conviction. They had somehow missed the gift, for it does not go inalienably with the production of offspring, and it is sometimes found in strange places—in the eyes of spinsters or invalids, in the smile of some whom the world despises.[53]

Thinly disguised as Amber, Webb first describes the cold, uncaring mother—a fitting depiction of Alice Meredith—and then herself, as spinster, invalid, and object of the world's scorn, as the better mother. Webb compares her mother to herself and finds herself superior. When describing Rachel Darke, Webb has control of her material; she can observe with some objectivity and freedom from rancor. "Mirth" is the word she chose to use here, for instance, rather than the more loaded possible terms "scorn" or "irony." But when it comes to the re-creation of herself on the page, such control is not entirely possible. And the rampant self-pitying glorification of self-sacrifice here cannot be missed.

Even after her marriage, the shyness and introversion Webb had learned as a young woman suffering the disfigurement of Graves' disease continued to hamper her. She was always ill at ease socially, and despite descriptions of her which make it clear that she was an attractive, energetic figure, she remained, at least in her own eyes, marred—and despised for that marring. The daughter may indeed be better than her mother, but the daughter is also a poor creature, a martyr, nearly a Quasimodo: monstrous, scorned, unwanted, but filled with feelings far more tender than the feelings of those who are accepted by the world and those who scorn her. This portrait of herself as the outcast who loves is to be found elsewhere in the novel, when for instance Amber comes upon a dying cow, "timid and wild," in a nearby field. The cow had strayed into the Wallows land, and because she was different from the big Herefords had been gored. Catherine wants to leave the bloody scene, but Amber kneels next to the cow to shield it from further goring, and waits for her brother to come and shoot it. Webb's "good" daughters are always associated with such vulnerability, and with the often small and always helpless creatures of the animal world. At the same time, such "good" daughters attempt to protect such helpless creatures, even at peril to their own lives. The "good" daughters are themselves weak in the world's terms but strong spiritually.

There is a reverse moralism in this presentation of the good daughter as one who is also likely to be gored. In this and in her other novels, Webb is eager to condemn the "herd mentality," the acceptance of the moral values and rules of behavior which a society mindlessly accepts and obeys. In all of her novels, Webb clearly sides with the forces of nature, of wood and beast and sky. Such forces are inexplicable and mysterious and often cruel, but they are also amoral. Nature's power is ferocious but real; society's power is real in its effects but no more than a series of artificially constructed precepts that an individual can deny if she so chooses—or so Webb would like to believe. In rejecting Christianity, Webb embraced instead a pagan mysticism that unites with the natural world and finds in the commonplace objects of woodland and farmyard instances of something far greater—godhead or world soul or deity. She experienced a pantheistic union with nature that resulted in her esteeming most those individuals who find inspiration and meaning apart from their culture. Some part of Webb knows that women cannot live whole and happily within society; she would like to believe that it is possible for them to live apart from society in union with nature, discovering its larger truth, its inexorable laws. Through this mystic union a woman can fulfill in safety her need for the merging of self—a need learned in her earliest childhood relationship with her mother. She can find, as well, a means by which the confines of the self can be undone without the danger that the loss of such boundaries entails when a woman merges with a man in the institutions of romance and marriage. Within nature, woman can resolve her dichotomous desires.

The spinster or invalid "whom the world despises" is not honored by Webb for her courage in breaking out of the social conventions that would circumvent her life and deny her passion, but loved for her weakness—she is loved *because* she is despised. She is the sanctified victim. Webb's vision and analysis of the domestic world and its forces are complex, but the emotions displayed concerning daughters are not. She presents the same posture, the same perspective, in this novel as she does in her poorer poetry, where she depicts herself as the lone child curled in the heart of a flower, watching the world go by. It is the pose of the adult who nourishes in her heart the wounded child—a wound she would prefer did not heal. We find some aspect of this wounded child present in the biographers' descriptions of Mary Webb at Lyth Hall, creeping into the hedges to watch the children at play. It is present in Hazel Woodus, the child of nature as victim, and in Deborah Arden, the long suffering, deserted, nearly grief-maddened wife. And we will find it in Rwth of *Seven for a Secret*.

Even as Webb seems intent on creating women who can achieve what they desire and yet not be cruel in that attainment, she also seems to need to sanctify women as victim—Hazel torn apart by dogs, Deborah deserted, Amber physically unattractive and somewhat too old for romance. Amber, to everyone's surprise and Catherine's bitter envy, does achieve the love she desires, and from the man who is clearly the most desirable of all, Michael Hallowes. Amber triumphs in love and over Catherine, who has always despised her. But concomitant with that victory in the novel's final romantic scene is Amber's self-abnegation before Michael Hallowes:

"Amber," said Michael, "what are you going to do with your life?"

"Give it to you and to—all this . . ."

"I have a confession to make, Amber."

She smiled and waited.

"These things may not content me. I knew it to-day. . . . Think of it! They and Arkinstall, your father, all of 'em, just the same, year by year. And out yonder—the world."

He looked at Amber keenly. The expression he had expected darted into her face—surprise, almost agony. So might a devout Catholic look, being excommunicated. Michael, watching her, wondered if she would pass the test. It was characteristic of him to test her thus, through pain. He was a hard man; hard to himself, to the world, hardest of all, perhaps, to the woman he loved. Not even on her wedding day did he spare her, chiefly because he so greatly wished to know how much she cared for him. . . .

She clasped her hands, hot with the stress of passion. For the love of nature is a passion for those in whom it once lodges. . . . It is a furious, burning, physical greed, as well as a state of mystical exaltation. It will have its own.

. . . She heard in her heart the individual leaf-song of every tree. These things were of her essence now. But Michael also was of the forest. These things belonged to her; but she belonged to Michael.

She looked up at last, and found his eyes on her. With a catch of the breath she said:

"Of course, Michael. We must go—away."[54]

In her acquiescence, Amber agrees to part from all that has held meaning for her; she agrees to give up the landscape and nature where she has experienced herself as an individual apart from her family's always thoughtless evaluation of her. Michael has asked her to follow him, and he is cognizant of what she will sacrifice in doing so. She will leave the cruelties of her growth in Dormer House, but she will also leave behind the woods where she came to know herself as whole and valuable. She gains a husband, but it is a husband who is gained, by his demand, at the cost of her landscape of self-discovery.

The melodrama of the scene and the sentimentality of the language is atypical of the otherwise tight and pointed prose of the rest of this novel. Throughout, Webb has been wry and ironic, and quick to note sham posturings and hypocrisy in the name of love. That Amber who had been the witty observant of others' foibles throughout her life at Dormer House now herself participates in the hyperventilated romance of this scene suggests that Webb cannot control the character who most resembles herself. And it suggests as well that while Webb is intent on depicting a means by which daughters can be powerful and maternal and kind, at the same time she would have the daughter willingly give up that power. Daughters can reject the dominating wills of their mothers, but if they love a man, then he must be willingly submitted to. The good daughter must learn to be victor over her mother and victim of her husband at the same time.

Seven for a Secret

The Dualism of Desire

The body stands for discontinuity, individuality, and life.
Consequently the violation of the body in erotic violation
breaks the taboo between life and death and breaks through
our discontinuity from the other. While this break is the
hidden secret of all eroticism, it is most clearly expressed
in erotic violation. The breakdown of the tension within
the individual between life and death, between assertion
and loss of self, occurs in the form of violator and violated.
One person maintains his or her boundary, and one allows
her or his boundary to be broken.

JESSICA BENJAMIN, *"Master and Slave: The Fantasy of Erotic*
Domination"

During the period 1921–1923, four important develop-
ments took place in Webb's life: she experienced writing difficulties for the first time; she made friends with various
London literati; her marriage began to suffer from severe
problems, which were never to be resolved; she began to in-
cur a series of debts that would plague her until her death.
Initially, Webb had been happy at Lyth Hill, but she now
became ill once again. Her doctor attributed this illness to her
lonely brooding and recommended a major change. Despite
his wife's unhappiness at leaving Shropshire, Henry persuaded her to move to London, where he had been offered a
post at a school he much preferred to his present position, in
which he found the boys dull and uninspiring. Henry also felt
that a move to London would help Mary get acquainted with
writers and critics who might be more inclined to notice her
work once she was no longer labeled "provincial."[1] Hence-
forth, Spring Cottage was to be used only as a vacation

home, as a place to return between school terms; it would remain so for the rest of Webb's life.

The move to London did, in fact, involve Webb in a larger cultural world. She sought and obtained reviewer work from the *Spectator,* the *Bookman,* and the *Nation;* these journals accepted her reviews, her essays, articles, and short stories.[2] She joined several literary clubs—P.E.N., the Bookman Circle, and the Tomorrow Club—and became friends with, among others, May Sinclair, Rebecca West, Sylvia Lynd, Caradoc Evans, and Edwin Pugh.[3] Still extremely shy, she made herself take part in musicales and plays at her various clubs. She read papers and presented her own work. Although the object of mockery by some of her female colleagues—Virginia Woolf and Vita Sackville-West, in particular, found her dress and behavior a source of snobbish mirth—Webb nonetheless made several close friends on whom she came to depend for help as her marriage and health began to decay.[4]

Despite her success at reviewing and writing, work on her fourth novel, *Seven for a Secret,* went not at all well. She now found that her usual rushes of inspiration—rushes which in the past had resulted in page after page of prose that required little revision—were happening with greater and greater infrequency. Coles may be correct when she attributes Webb's writing block, at least in part, to the move from Lyth Hill to London; Webb's modest success in the London literary scene was not enough to make up for her loss of Spring Cottage and the Shropshire landscape, where she had been accustomed to writing outdoors during as much of the year as possible. Even when forced indoors she still could see her garden and the surrounding hills. But from neither of the London flats the Webbs occupied during this period was she able to see anything resembling countryside. And, in fact, in one flat she discovered her garden raided of every bud and flower on three separate occasions—flower sellers had gotten there early in the morning and stripped the entire area bare.[5]

She felt claustrophobic in London with Henry and could not write, yet her short trips to Spring Cottage in hope that a return to familiar landscape could help her writing were unproductive because she suffered such great anxiety in Henry's absence. For some reason, the move to London had caused her great insecurity. She was no longer sure that her husband was faithful to her or that he was even where he said he was. She began following him to school, calling him and even unexpectedly showing up in the common room. At Spring Cottage she brooded continually over the possibility that he was betraying her, yet when Henry accompanied her to the cottage for a weekend, she argued with him. The quarrels at times became so bitter that Henry would return early to London, a move that only increased Webb's fears of his unfaithfulness.[6] There seems to be no evidence that Henry was anything other than loyal during this period, though he was later to become quite infatuated with a young woman whom he tutored, the same young woman whom, after Mary Webb's death, he was to marry. But while he was faithful during this period, he had begun to lose patience. Quite well liked at his new school, admired by both his pupils and colleagues, who found him an innovative teacher, he appreciated neither his wife's dogged attention nor her surprise appearances on the most flimsy of pretexts.

Webb's health began to worsen in London. Her goiter increased and her hands noticeably shook. She was very thin. Although treatment had recently become available for the pernicious anemia that ultimately killed her and for Graves' disease, Webb refused all medical attention. Rebecca West, unable to watch the unheeded physical destruction which the disease caused, eventually found friendship with Webb too difficult to maintain. While the two women continued to correspond, West began to find excuses not to meet with her.[7] Webb seemed bent on killing herself with neglect, and through her poor diet did quite literally hasten her own death. Always a vegetarian, Webb would have a difficult time obtaining adequate amounts of iron; her overstimulated thyroid, in addition, demanded great amounts of food for her increased metabolism. Nevertheless, she seemed to exist mainly on tea, bread, butter, and jam.

But even as she skimped on her own food—and on Henry's

as well—the inordinate generosity that had caused her to give pianos to the children of Lyth Hill now caused her to take on whole families from London's tenements. Coles sees the origin of Webb's philanthropy in her guilt at having spent the war years safe and happy in the countryside while so many men were suffering on the front and so many families were enduring the privation of the wartime city, and she suggests that Webb was undergoing a form of "survivor's guilt" that caused her to suffer now since she had not suffered earlier. Coles expresses an unhappy surprise that some did not understand or approve of Webb's wholehearted generosity, but interpreted her actions as erratic, even unbalanced.[8] But how else is one to judge a philanthropy that had Webb serving tea and stale bread for supper, while begging publishers for advance money, accepting large "loans" from rich, anonymous donors, and hoarding royalties and reviewer fees so that she might send an entire family to the seaside for a week? The vacationing family was most grateful, although after they arrived they wrote complaining of a lack of funds. Webb obligingly sent more money. When she went to visit the family after their return, she discovered that the money had been used to purchase various articles which they had, in turn, sold for a small profit. That single event did not sour her generous impulses, but neither did it make her wiser in giving.[9]

Webb continued to write alternately whining and angry letters to her publisher, letters in which she suggested that she was being cheated of her full royalty payments, and which described the poor fare she was forced to eat. Yet when money was forthcoming, it was used for others. It is hardly an exaggeration to claim, as does Barbara Hannah, that Webb did more than give away money; she gave away, as well, her own life.[10]

Webb was debt-ridden, anxious over her husband and marriage, and continually moving from London to Spring Cottage and back again, and within London, from flat to flat. She was physically ill and, by her own account, nearly starving, yet driven to take upon herself the monetary needs of every stranger who came to her door. Each condition is in itself overwhelming; interrelated they are fatal. And all these daily conditions *were* interrelated, each affecting and effecting the other. Her money problems forced her to take on more and more reviewing work which took time from her novel. While her reviewing did make her known among some of London's writers, she suffered terribly from their real and imagined snubbings, and her paranoia increased. Her writing difficulties would then make her return to Spring Cottage in hopes of greater productivity, but the separation served to inflame her anxieties about Henry's love. Back in London, she nagged Henry so much that he did, in fact, begin to distance himself from her. As his wife became more frustrated with her writing and more insecure in her marriage, Henry found increasingly more to do at school.[11] And it seemed that the greater their money problems, the more inclined Webb was to play philanthropist.

★   ★   ★

Seven for a Secret was finally completed during the winter of 1921. It won the approval of her literary contemporaries and gained far more attention than had any of her previous books. The comments were considerably more favorable than those which had greeted *The House in Dormer Forest* two years earlier. Perhaps Henry's suggestion that London friends and a London address might remove the label of "provincial" had indeed proven wise, or perhaps the time was simply right. At any rate, American critical response was enthusiastic. And although the actual number of copies sold was not appreciably greater than that of her earlier novels, her reputation grew among London's literary circles. Some small measure of the fame for which she was so very desperate was now coming her way.

Despite the novel's popularity, the three major critics who have dealt with it consider it to be one of lesser worth. Gladys Coles believes that the novel is flawed by the fact that Gillian Lovekin, its principal character, is not a mystic; thus the novel never moves beyond a single level of meaning, since it is not a moral fable, nor does it have symbolic meaning and multiple suggestion.[12] She suggests that Webb was trying to write "a different kind of novel, blending satire, fantasy and fable" and that she had deliberately intended to write a "fabulous tale" that would seem to be nearly "a parody of her own previous work."[13] Glen Cavaliero, on the other hand, finds *Seven for a Secret* pleasantly free from the heavy didacticism that characterized her other novels, but still weak in its repetition of certain situations, conflicts, and characters found in her earlier work. The novel, he says, was not "a fabulous tale" but rather attempted too much, investing its straightforward narrative with a "spurious significance." Its portentousness could not be sustained and thus its climax was "half-hearted," unable to meet the demands made on it in the novel's earlier parts. Cavaliero finds evidence of a "disintegrated imagination" that can no longer create but only repeat.[14] Dorothy Wrenn finds the novel highly symbolic, filled with characters like those of a morality play or allegory.[15] She compares the novel to *Wuthering Heights,* not in terms of greatness, but in its purposeful use of exaggeration of plot and character. As with *Wuthering Heights, Seven for a Secret* was written during a profoundly emotional period of the author's life, and Wrenn believes that evidence of those feelings can be traced within the novel itself. Thus the critics are at odds, Coles faulting the book for a lack of symbolic significance, Cavaliero criticizing it for attempting to convey too much significance. Wrenn sees the novel as reflecting Webb's psyche, but Coles says there is no resemblance between Gillian and Webb since Gillian is incapable of mysticism. In fact, Coles would suggest that Robert Rideout, Gillian's shepherd-lover, shares the novel with her as principal character, since it is he who is passionate and mystical, suffering and poetic.[16] But Cavaliero believes that the presence of Robert Rideout contributes to what Cavaliero describes as the novel's "soft" sensibility, since it is precisely Rideout's kinship with the moors and his poetizing that burdens the novel with significance it cannot sustain.[17] Wrenn, viewing the novel as allegory, sees each of its four central characters as facets of Webb's personality:

Rwth—inarticulateness; Robert Rideout—tenderness; Ralph Elmer—possessiveness; and Gillian—lack of understanding.[18]

It is not all surprising that such close readers as these cannot agree on the novel's merits and faults. *Seven for a Secret,* as the title states, is about mystery—and although the most obvious secrets are revealed and the most evident mysteries solved, the novel ends on a purposely ambiguous note. Webb poses a series of questions and then, pointedly, does not answer them. The unsolved mysteries and unanswered questions have to do with the problem of intentionality in the universe. Why do some suffer while others are happy? Is death end or union? Can we ever understand the meaning of events? Why does human growth demand suffering? Is history random or directed? The novel's narrator seems to suggest that with death comes union and therefore understanding. But the events of the novel suggest that it is mere accident that some die so that others can live and be happy. The novel's conclusion further suggests that all efforts to circumvent the final anonymity of death—except through the reproduction of offspring—fail. There is only biological immortality, at least for women.[19] And even that immortality is not personal since women lose their names and take their husbands'. Thus the novel is intentionally a mystery, and purposely enigmatic. Diversity of interpretation is understandable.

Another reason might explain such diversity among the novel's critics. *Seven for a Secret* reflects the divided desire of its author—and of women in general. Webb longs for autonomy but seeks domination. She acknowledges the pain of her oppression even as she desires union with the oppressor. She would be free from society's constructions of the female and yet achieve fame and acknowledgment within that society. And finally, she would articulate the fact of her oppression and the forces which deny the story of that oppression, but she will also have the teller of that story murdered. Such warring desires result in a novel of blunted force and blurred intent. It is not that she tells a truth and a lie, but that she tells

two true tales which contradict each other, and cannot find
their mutual source.

★   ★   ★

Webb's divided desire is reflected in the novel's two female
characters: Gillian, who longs for autonomy, and Rwth, who
is the embodiment of selfless love. Yet the stories of the two
women are integrally entwined, and each woman becomes—
Gillian permanently, and Rwth momentarily—through the
effect of the other, what she has not previously been. Gillian
finds subservient love in Robert's arms and Rwth rebelliously
tells how her passive submission has been forced through
male brutality. Thus each woman represents one half of
Webb's desire—autonomy and passivity—yet each embodies
at the same time desire's other face. When Gillian learns to
love as a mature woman ought, she abrogates her longing for
self-determination, her desire for fame and immortality, and
chooses to merge her own identity with that of her husband.
But when Gillian teaches the mute Rwth to write, the story
of the dominating males' role in creating subservient women
is made clear: female self-sacrifice is at best taught and at
worst enforced; it is the product of fear rather than choice.
The novel as a whole and its concluding paragraph in particular make it clear to the reader that "good" and "wise" and
"happily mature" women choose wifely submission. The
novel's secret tale reveals that the sacrifice of autonomy is the
price that must be paid if a woman is to live at all. Women,
in other words, will function most contentedly within society if they agree to society's demands. Their rewards will be
the joys—and power—of wifehood and maternity. Women,
nonetheless, desire the freedom of self-determination; they
seek to grow and create themselves for their own ends rather
than form themselves to the constructed roles and lives of
their society. For this desire there is no reward; there is only
danger.

Seven for a Secret tells two contradictory stories: that of
woman aiding woman so the truth of women's oppression
may be revealed, and that of woman as the slave of love who

must learn through pain the lesson of her true nature—that she is destined to be the submissive, maternal partner to the dominant male. The novel, in other words, depicts the horror, despair, and brutality of male oppression even as it affirms female submission. Both of these stories are rendered in the diction of a religious mysticism whose emphasis on union and the consequent loss of self serve to beatify further the sacrifice of a woman's autonomy. Woman is biologically destined to submit her freedom to the demands of wifehood and maternity; since such is *nature's* plan, she must acquiesce or remain free but unfulfilled. *Seven for a Secret* presents both a romantic tale of submission and a covert tale of dominance.

Telling such tales, *Seven for a Secret* has a clear parallel with the literature of sexual domination. It tells a flowery, quasi-mystical, yet vaguely titillating story of the relationship between the sexes, of the ways by which a woman comes to know her true "nature," and in what that female "nature" consists. That such a narrative is the typical one of women's romance novels only suggests that while the guises may be various, the need to explore an unchanging model of heterosexual relationships is great.[20] How a woman relates to a man and what it is that she learns about herself from that relationship are the overt issues of the romantic novel. But the covert questions of these novels—questions unarticulated but nonetheless present—concern the very nature of female desire itself. Woman's need for autonomy and the fact that her autonomy exists in tandem with her need for union with another being are the hidden issues of this and other romantic tales told by women.

Webb's first three novels give evidence of her belief in the rightness of female self-abnegation. Amber will sacrifice all for love; Deborah shows herself the willing and able student of such a lesson. Hazel, alone, never actually makes the choice to abrogate her own desires. Marston, at *Gone to Earth's* end, offers her the chance to make right the wrongs *he* has suffered—she can marry him and bear *his* son—by forsaking her childish longing to live apart from the world's demands. But

Hazel dies before she agrees to his offer. Yet even with Hazel, and certainly with Deborah and Amber, Webb demonstrates that *woman's* lesson of love is to learn to subdue her own desires, ambitions, and individuality. The reward for such womanly education, of course, is husband and child.

The way in which a woman learns this lesson—subjugation—as well as what she learns—wifehood and maternity—bear close resemblance to various psychoanalytic models of female sexual development that posit anatomy as destiny and female acquiescence as natural. Such depictions of female growth imply that subservience is woman's biologically determined posture; to be subdued is the process of her maturation. Woman is, therefore, the natural masochist. While she may neither enact nor desire instances of physical pain, she does seek a life of domination. The literature of submission and domination merely exaggerates the supposed process and nature of female desire, making the physical acts metaphor for psychological fact. Steven Marcus, in his study of nineteenth-century British pornography, outlines the shape common to tales of master/slave sexuality:

Each begins with a virgin, reluctant, proud, chaste, a woman in whom Nature has not yet been awakened. She then undergoes a series of violent experiences, which usually include beating, flogging, and defloration in the form of rape. By means of these sufferings her pride is subdued, her chastity broken, and in their place Nature—responsiveness—is substituted.[21]

Reading *Seven for a Secret* with Marcus's synoptic model in mind, we see that Gillian and Rwth undergo the same "womanly" lesson, one physically and the other emotionally. One is stolen, raped, beaten, and humiliated; she is the unwilling victim who nonetheless learns through her suffering "the secret that's never been told." The other is the willing victim, initially willing because of her own sexual curiosity, but ultimately willing because of her love; she learns the "triumphant beauty of wifehood and motherhood" when she is finally able to relinquish all desire for fame, power, and autonomy. What each woman learns differently in kind but not in fact is that female nature is happiest when dominated, that such is the nature of mature relations between the sexes. Each woman learns her lesson in acceptance of this fact through the act of male domination. And what each woman learns is that her identity is to have none. Rwth may hate her treatment at Ralph and Fringal's hands—and Webb makes it quite clear that we are not to believe that such mistreatment is noble or good—but she adores Robert, worships even his belongings, and is happiest when she can polish his booted feet. Gillian may despise Ralph, but her seduction and subsequent unhappy marriage to him are the painful but necessary lessons that enable her to sacrifice herself to Robert's domination. Women learn their true identity through male brutalization—physical and emotional—and what they learn about their identity is that it exists to die, metaphorically or literally.

Submission in the blatantly sexual tale rewards the woman with sexual pleasure, with sensations forbidden her by society and unavailable to her as virgin. She must be violently "taken" and brutally "used" before she can experience her own sexuality. Only then can she know her own true "nature," which is not merely one of submission but of the sexual ecstasy to be found in that submission. She submits and thereby learns to submerge herself in rapture. Submission in the romantic tale and in this novel is not nearly so blatantly sexual, although Robert's so-called love poem is a thinly veiled sadistic fantasy of a Gillian who will lie at his feet, beg for love, her hair spread out about her on the floor, a woman made breathless by his kisses.[22] Such a depiction of love as subjugation seems only a more covert version of those stories in which a prostrate female begs the physically dominant male to "do it" to her. In romantic novels it is love rather than the whip that dominates. Further examination of *Seven for a Secret* illustrates the contradictory tales Webb creates as mirrors of her own—and women's—socialized, coexistent desires for, at best, independence and union, for, at worst, autonomy and dominance.

* ★ *

Impetuous and stubborn, Gillian is determined to leave her father's farm and see life; her musicianship will be her financial means to attain this freedom. The single drawback to her grand plan is that Gillian has never learned any music, but she nonetheless remains certain that such a scheme is possible for her. This adolescent Gillian is neither passive nor doom-ladened. Early in the novel, just after Gillian has declared her intentions of winning money, silk gowns, applause, and a host of adoring suitors among whom she can choose and reject, Gillian stands in her father's pasture. She has been trapping rabbits to sell their pelts for money for music lessons; not even harmless creatures are safe in the face of Gillian's ambition. As she stands there, the dead booty at her feet, splashed with their blood, the sheep stir about her "like uneasy souls," while the rabbits lying at her feet seem like a sacrifice to some woodland goddess.[23] Silvered in the moonlight, Gillian is described in terms of the crescent moon: she is slender, "sharp," and "cutting." Webb further compares Gillian to a ruthlessly pursuing falcon, supple, sure, and deadly powerful. Neither in Gillian's posture nor in these comparisons of her to moon and predator is there the least suggestion of feminine gentleness. Nor is her bloodstained dress suggestive of future doom. The scar on Gillian's forehead that will disappear upon her acceptance of wifehood and maternity is, at this time, "shining" and "relentless" in the moonlight. The intended effect of this description is one of sharp cruelty and bloody death. This young Gillian is the Artemis of the silvered crescent moon and killing arrow. But by the novel's conclusion Gillian has changed from the huntress to the mother, from Artemis to Demeter. The rationale for such change is, as in *Gone to Earth*, the necessary capitulation demanded by nature of all creatures: that they mate and reproduce.

Using a theme previously employed in *Gone to Earth*, spiritual versus carnal love, Webb has Gillian sought after by Robert Rideout, her father's herdsman and therefore an unworthy suitor who has been forbidden to court her, and also by Ralph Elmer, a horse trader of seeming ambition and wealth. However, in true fairy-tale fashion, Robert is unworthy of Gillian only because of his station in life. In fact, he is a sensitive would-be poet who has known Gillian all her life and who best loves and understands her wild nature. When Gillian goes to Silverton to visit her Aunts Fanteague and Emily and, her father hopes, to learn womanly refinements and meet eligible young men, Robert makes arrangements with his friend, Gipsy Johnson, to watch the girl and make sure that no harm comes to her. But Gillian's determination is no match, even for Gipsy Johnson. She manages to meet and ultimately spend the night with Ralph Elmer, whose blatant sexual interest in her has aroused her own curiosity. When she awakens next to Ralph in the morning, Gillian is "angry and ashamed and scornful" of the great mystery that surrounds sex, and she is suddenly very aware that it is Robert she loves and not Ralph Elmer:

So this was all that lay behind the locked and guarded door that the matrons kept so carefully! This was the secret that she had given her maidenhood to discover! No, this was not all. There was no love in it, and so it was a lamp unlit. If Robert had awakened by her side—[24]

A few moments after this realization of her mistake, Gillian's father and Robert arrive at the inn where the couple have spent the night. Despite her certainty that she does not love Ralph, Gillian is made to marry him.

This part of the plot is the stuff of potboiler romance and second-rate fiction. The working-out of the novel's conclusion is little better. Ralph Elmer has two servants, the sour Fringal and the mute Rwth who, having been shown kindness by Robert Rideout, becomes his silent worshiper. Robert is suspicious of Rwth's presence in the house but her muteness makes it impossible to question her. He decides that Gillian must teach Rwth to read and write so that something about her background can be discovered. Gipsy Johnson's baby daughter, Ailse, had been kidnaped many years before; Robert suspects that Rwth and Ailse are the same person.

What Robert does not immediately suspect is that not only is Rwth Ailse, but Rwth is Ralph Elmer's wife, and Elmer's marriage to Gillian is therefore invalid. When Elmer begins to suspect that his bigamy is about to be revealed, he murders Rwth and buries her in the snow. Robert has followed Elmer, but arrives too late to save her.

Gillian and Robert are now free to marry. At the novel's end there is a flash-forward, and we see Gillian as the joyful mother of a boy and girl who discuss their mother's great happiness. We are informed by the narrator that Gillian has forsaken her ambitions for fame and immortality, and is now content to share in whatever immortality comes in the production of children. Gillian is happy to be known simply as Robert the herdsman's wife.

While the story allows its reader to enjoy a bit of passion and romance and illicit sex, it ends by reaffirming the social values of love and marriage and motherhood. It elevates to great moral heights the protective instincts of the male for his beloved. And in its beatification of Rwth, the novel makes self-abnegation, even unto death, an act far more virtuous than Gillian's maternal self-sacrifice. Thus the simple mysteries—who is Rwth? where is Gipsy Johnson's lost daughter? what is the secret of Ralph Elmer's hidden past?—are solved, and the choice between love and carnality is properly made. The joys of maternal love are shown to be preferable to the power and immortality of artistic fame, but the mystic's goal of her complete loss of self in union with the whole is shown to be most valuable of all:

Maybe it was not Gillian, in all the tremulous yet triumphant beauty of wifehood and motherhood, not even Robert in the glory of manhood and poetry and courageous love that came nearest to this mystery, which decrees that those who are all love, as Ailse was, must suffer, while those who are selfish, like Gillian, are redeemed. Perhaps it was Ailse's compensation, as she floated downstream to eternity in the water-lily of a pure and unrewarded love, that she understood before them all the secret that's never been told.[25]

The implication of this passage, the very last of the novel, is that the secret which has never been told can only be fully revealed through a mystical experience. Yet the whole shape of the novel, as well as its conclusion, suggests that an entirely different secret is being hinted at—but not being told: that Webb herself prefers fame and immortality to domestic bliss, and that she would punish such a desire even as she enacts it. Webb initially creates a heroine who is callow but passionate, who is curious, intelligent, selfish, and aggressive, whose zest for life and developing sexuality result in the death—from a fatal chest cold—of her aunt's longtime suitor. By the novel's conclusion, Webb has not had Gillian satisfy her longings and so grow quieter. Rather she has taken from Gillian the very qualities that most defined her: a desire for independence, a yearning to be allowed to be herself. Ralph Elmer was brutal and dominated both Rwth and Gillian through fear. Robert Rideout, like Michael Hallowes, will dominate by means of Gillian's love.

*   *   *

Thus, through the novel's actions, Gillian's desire and power are lessened; Gillian is reduced rather than allowed to grow. Webb does this because she fears the creation of a female character such as Gillian. A Gillian who does not capitulate to love, marriage, and maternity is far too powerful an image; she is the successful daughter whom Webb both wanted to be and yet feared to become. Amber Darke was the passive observer of life until Michael Hallowes's appearance. Then her love for him enabled her to perform the outrageous act of going alone to his cottage and spending the night. Amber did not need to be tamed; she already was. Hazel Woodus's passionate desire for freedom from domesticity was always shadowed by our knowledge that she was doomed. Webb created a character such as Gillian because of her need to fashion a daughter neither timid like Amber nor doomed like Hazel. But having created such a daughter, she then feared her.

During this period of her life, Webb was highly anxious to achieve her own fame and fortune; she wished literary acknowledgment, and several of her friends speculated that the illness which caused Henry to suggest the move to London was a product of Webb's intense depression at the limited success of *The House in Dormer Forest*. Gillian's desires are callow, as might be expected of an adolescent, but her gowns and suitors mirror rather well her creator's desire for renown, acclaim, applause, audience. Having created a character who reflects those needs, Webb then punished Gillian for those very desires.

Writing had enabled Webb to create a character who could both achieve and be punished for what her author desired. The roles of mystic and the financially successful author are difficult to unite, just as it is hard to reject the mother's use of power while affirming the daughter's right to power. How, in other words, could a daughter have power and not be just like her mother? Both Deborah Arden and Amber Darke abrogate all personal power and desire in the name of love; they give up self and become lover and wife. Hazel Woodus was unable to make that sacrifice and so died. Gillian Lovekin is an attempt to grapple once again with the exact same problem of daughterhood, only this time the heroine is strong and self-assertive. Webb lets Gillian live, but she "clips her wings" as would Robert. Gillian's "fame" will be Robert's creation; she will be remembered as the subject of his love songs and as the mother of the children he will give her. Neither Robert nor Webb see any injustice in this. Robert's desire to domesticate and subordinate Gillian mirrors that of Webb. It is the poets—Robert and Webb—who unmake Gillian the huntress and would-be artist.

Like Gillian, Rwth embodies a part of Webb's divided desire. Rwth as servant, as Robert's adorer, as abused, neglected, sweet and gentle woman passively accepting her fate, exemplifies Webb's model lover; she is the mystic soul. Webb can reflect her own desire for autonomy and independent achievement through the character of Gillian. And with Rwth she can reflect her need to be the good and submissive daughter and wife. Rwth is the daughter who gives all she has. And because Rwth is a martyr, she is also saint. But in

the story of Rwth's writing lessons there is another story as
well, the feminist one. And it is this story that is the real secret
of *Seven for a Secret*.

★ ★ ★

In *Gone to Earth* Webb created a short but significant scene
in which one woman crudely but kindly offers aid to another;
Sally Haggard and Hazel momentarily unite against Jack Reddin's brutality. In *Seven for a Secret* such female bonding again
occurs, but this time at length. The result of this bond between Gillian and Rwth is the unraveling of the mystery of
Rwth's identity as daughter, wife, and mother. Rwth's real
name and her hidden history are revealed because Gillian
teaches her to write. This theme of the power of literacy is
begun in *Seven for a Secret* and developed fully in *Precious
Bane*.

At Robert's suggestion, Gillian teaches Rwth to write the
name of her gypsy mother, Esmeralda. One day, having written Esmeralda three times, Rwth laboriously writes the name
Ailse, the country form of the name Alice and her own original name. The name means nothing to Gillian, who is ignorant of Robert's intentions in having Rwth learn to write.
But Robert recognizes immediately that Rwth is the lost child
of Gipsy Johnson. Robert is awed by Rwth's ability to re-
member her true name, "for this was the memory of a bird,
of a squirrel, memory untaught and expressing itself with the
utmost difficulty."[26] The linking of Rwth with the creatures
of nature suggests that we are to view her as an example of
the "natural" woman—one who can, therefore, love selflessly, mystically, because she has not been perverted by selfish desires, as has Gillian. But the novel's events make it clear
that the distinction between selfless love and being a "slave of
love" is not especially great.

Writing will enable Rwth to recover what seemingly had
been lost: her own childhood history, her life before kidnap-
ing and subsequent servitude to Ralph Elmer:

He gazed and gazed upon the impassive face of Rwth, who was
Ailse—of Rwth the maid-of-all-work who was the daughter of a

kind of gipsy-king—of Ailse who had prattled in gipsy merriment
and who was now Rwth the dumb girl—of Ailse the child of sweet
love, the child of a woman like a star, who was, or had been till
Gillian's advent, the dumb foundling dependent on Elmer's charity,
the creature that, Robert shrewdly suspected, knew what it was to
be beaten.[27]

Writing ultimately enables Rwth to reveal the whole of her
brutalized life. She had been kidnaped by Ralph's servant
Fringal, who, after some years had passed, forced Ralph Elmer to marry the girl lest the neighbors gossip:

"You're a cunning old man," said Ralph. "I dunna forget as it was
you that made me marry the nasty little thing."
    "You was quite content till the t'other [Gillian] turned up."
    "I made the best of it."
    "But it were a pity we didna get a doctor when the brat was
born. And then you clouting the girl after, and telling her too soon
about it being dead—"
    "She wore me out, moaning for it."[28]

As in a fairy tale, the foundling Ailse is in fact the child of a
noble father and a beautiful mother, kidnaped and sold into
bondage. But the true story of her silence is far too brutal,
and far too realistic, even for a fairy tale. Beaten after giving
birth unattended, she learns that her child is dead; Rwth is
mute thereafter.

One day, with Gillian in one room and Robert watching
from another, Rwth performs an act of deliberate and dangerous defiance. She uncovers the blackboard on which she
had practiced her letters, and in clear view of Fringal and
Ralph Elmer begins to write the tale of her past. When he
recovers from his shock, Fringal suggests a solution: "Canna
you see . . . she's mad. She can write, but she's mad. She
mun go to the asylum."[29] Ralph readily agrees. He will have
her put away. No one will believe the rantings of a madwoman. Gillian enters the room and is informed that Rwth
has gone mad and is to be shut up. Gillian refuses to permit
this, and promises to find out what it was on the now erased
blackboard that has so upset her husband. Rwth, she tells

him, will stay, and she will continue to write: "You've got a tidy bit to hide, seemingly . . . if you're so terrified of what poor Rwth writes."[30] All night Elmer and Fringal debate what to do. The next day Ralph threatens Rwth: "If you dare to write any more I'll pretty nigh kill ye!"[31] But Rwth merely stares at her husband with defiance. She loves Robert and at his request will not reveal to Gillian that she is married to Elmer. But she will write anything that Robert requests; she will tell Gillian as much as she can. Fringal expresses the hope that Rwth will sicken and die, but Ralph knows that real action is necessary. He begins to plan her murder.

That afternoon Rwth goes to the forest where she has built a bower of branches. There she has placed the little treasures that Robert has given her: a handkerchief, a pencil, a flower. She nearly worships these: "On festivals she came and took them out and adored them. Her lifted face was enraptured," as she whispered aloud, "Robert Rideout! Robert Rideout!"[32] But Ralph is nearby, a gun in one hand, a brace of rabbits in the other. He hears her, realizes she will no longer remain mute, and hears a whisper as well "from somewhere, from nowhere, out of the earth or the pallid sky, or out of Fringal's bleak mind"—the spirit of evil.[33] Ralph raises his gun and shoots Rwth. Robert is also nearby and comes upon Ralph strangely sweaty in the cold and growing dark of evening. Robert inquires about Rwth's whereabouts, and Ralph tells him that Rwth has run away. Robert has doubts, but cannot prove otherwise. Robert goes his way for a time, but then turns back to the Gyland where he had expected to find Rwth that afternoon. He hears the sound of digging in the dark, and watches Ralph in the moonlight bury something in the deep snow. Robert is certain it is Rwth's body.

As silent in dying as she had been in living, "Rwth fell forward without a sound. She slipped into eternity within the globing peace of her love, as the chrysalis of a dragon-fly might go down-stream in a water-lily."[34] This description of Rwth's death seems oddly lyrical considering the fact that she has been murdered, but then, this is a novel filled with discrepancies and contradiction. Gillian is both punished and rewarded in that wife and motherhood replace fame and fortune. On an even deeper level than this substitution of one set of pleasures for another, Gillian's desire for personal immortality through art is sacrificed for the biological immortality of progeny. And Rwth, too, is both punished and rewarded: she is murdered, but, we are assured, she is now privy to the greater insight gained through her union with nature. Rwth gains the personal immortality Gillian has lost, but Rwth had to die to be rewarded. Rwth thus embodies, as does Gillian, Webb's divided desire.

★ ★ ★

The cause of Rwth's punishment is her memory of her childhood and the injustices done her. Her expression of this knowledge causes Ralph Elmer first to declare her mad, and then to kill her when her sanity is defended and his own motives questioned. Rwth's character, her roles of stolen child, abused wife, student and subsequent writer of history, and her fate—all seem to be a portrait of the author as female. Yet how peculiar an insertion this portrait seems in light of this particular novel, which not only punishes the strong woman but rewards even the self-sacrificing woman with murder. In the very center of such a woman-negating tale is this other— a tale in which a woman teaches, befriends, and defends another woman, in which a woman remembers the mother from whom she has been stolen, in which a woman is made mute by a husband's abuse, but is taught language and hence a means of accusation by another woman. And it is not insignificant that both women are married to the same brutal man and that both women love the same gentle man: the fate of each is inextricably bound to the other's. The safety of one and the happiness of the other are entwined. This is exactly the portrait of the bonds of sisterhood that modern feminists posit, whether writing literary criticism or political theory.

Thus, literacy enables hidden truths to emerge—in particular, the lost history of a woman made mute by her own brutalized life. The previously unspoken is at last articulated.

It is not difficult to see the novel's plot as metaphor for the emergence of Webb's sense of authorship as the agent which enables her own history to be told—disguised and changed in form, fiction's factuality. The history that is revealed in Rwth's case is one that shows a daughter's sexual vulnerability when deprived of parental protection, her resultant silence in the face of her continued mistreatment, and male invalidation of her words when finally another woman gives her a means of statement. To our knowledge, Webb was not physically or sexually abused as a child; she was not made literally mute by the events of her life; her novels, though limited in their success, were not critically invalidated. So what then is the connection between Webb's story of Rwth and Webb's own story?

Webb must have perceived herself as abandoned, certainly by her father, who did not prevent Alice's return to the parlor as mistress, but also by her mother, whose time and attention were necessarily removed from her eldest daughter and directed to the next five children born between Webb's sixth and thirteenth year. While George Meredith may have encouraged his daughter's intellectual growth, to what purpose? What female child of a century ago would not correctly perceive her social worth as existing in areas quite other than those of her creative imagination? The lost Eden upon which Webb's biographers and critics place so much emphasis represented not merely the universal loss of childhood's freedom, but the universal female experience in which the girl child learns that she is "other" and "alien" and that her desires and self-value are denied validity by the world beyond Eden's gates. Boy children grow up learning that to speak is their privilege; girl children grow up learning not to speak. Webb married a man who valued her talents, who knew that darned socks and clean dishes were secondary to novels and thought. The problems in the Webb marriage, evidence would seem to indicate, arose from issues other than a woman's fight for time to create. But a good husband is not enough to rectify the loss experienced with girlhood's early realization: the knowledge that what she speaks has no worth, that when she speaks she is not heard, that all her truths and perceptions are qualified by the pejorating adjective "woman's."

One aspect of Webb's kinship with Rwth exists in their mutual sexual vulnerability. Rwth's vulnerability was physical; her woman's body was harmed because she lacked parental protection. Webb's wound was internal, and no parent could protect her from the knowledge that it was her gender, her woman's body and mind, which was the cause of her pain. This is Webb's hidden history enunciated through Rwth, the sainted victim. Webb lost her mother to her siblings and her father to her mother. But even if she had not lost them in this variation of the psychoanalytic paradigm— even if Alice had not been cold and critical and George not willing to resume his proper husbandly relationship with his wife—they yet could be no safeguard against the female child's recognition of her devaluation and muting by and within her society. Rwth reflects also, perhaps, that part of Webb which cannot help but tell the truth of her injuries and loss—even if the act of telling will kill her. Gillian is the never-developed artist, but Rwth *is* a successful author of her own story. And it is a story that, once told, makes possible Gillian's happy marriage and maternity. The awful tale finally told results in birth—though in this novel it is purely biological birth rather than artistic growth and creation.

Gillian is the embryonic artist who is never born; Robert Rideout is the poet, but a poet whose songs all deal with his love for Gillian and his need to dominate her. Rwth is the mute whose story-telling is the final truth—the truth both in terms of the plot's resolution and the truth that cannot be told. The tale Rwth tells is like no tale that Webb tells in any of the novels so far considered. It is a story that is not, it would appear, autobiographically accurate for Webb, but that is culturally accurate for her gender. It is the tale of a dominating patriarchy that not only steals daughters from the maternal body, but steals daughters from their maternal history. It is a tale in which even the act of birth is dominated by males. It is a tale that, when revealed, is called insane by men—because its truth is damning. And it is a tale that can be written only because one woman aids another—because, in other words, a woman has learned and so can teach another what had been forbidden.

Even as Webb attempted to write a novel in which she punished her selfish tendencies and all those impulses that were not maternal, were not wifely, and even as she attempted to show that self-sacrifice is the best act a woman can perform, Webb wrote the tale she didn't want to tell, despite her desire to be mute. She wrote a story that seems so disparate with her own biography that we could easily dismiss it as sheer authorial ineptitude spawning a need for plot-complexity, were the story not one found elsewhere and often in the writing of women authors.

Over and over again we have seen Webb justify female subordination and self-sacrifice because of biology: nature demands the perpetuation of the species, and women must submit to this demand or, like Hazel, die. For Webb, woman's sexuality and love are inextricably bound. The sacrifice of the self was sweetened in each case by the fact of love. Amber and Deborah willingly gave themselves and their futures to their husbands; Hazel, finally realizing the futility of her struggle, might have been willing to give up her freedom, but it was too late. Gillian loses both her station and her name, but is happy as the herdsman's wife. The reward for each woman's submission is her husband's love. Lost in their husbands, these women enact on a lesser scale the mystic's achievement of loss of the self in the whole. The patriarchy is continued and affirmed—by woman herself—and the reasons for doing so are made blessed because they imitate the mystical. The daughter's failure to achieve her goal is made a holy act rather than an act that might inspire despair or anger. This is, in a sense, the creation of a new language, a renaming of parts. The powerless woman becomes the good woman. The dominating male becomes the Universe in which the passive mystic loses herself to find her real happiness, like Ailse, dead but happiest of all.

The final secret Webb so covertly discloses involves that

strange and too familiar dichotomous state in which the woman's desire for subjugation coexists with the desire for sovereignty. Her longing self must be renounced. And yet— the tale must nonetheless be told. The need for articulation cannot be denied.

Precious Bane

A Daughter as Author of Herself

The novel is that creation by the woman of the woman.
JULIET MITCHELL, *"Femininity, Narrative and Psychoanalysis"*

The last four years of Mary Webb's life—1923–1927—were characterized by loss. The period begins with the completion of her best novel, *Precious Bane,* written in three months during the late summer and early autumn of 1923, and ends with her death in 1927, her weakest novel, *Armour Wherein He Trusted,* half completed, the manuscript singed by the fire in which she attempted to destroy it. Her death at forty-six was not a tragic end to a life filled with grand and passionate gestures prematurely concluded by universal fate. Webb's last years were filled with the trivialities that burden even the dying. As her disease progressed, she wasted herself in equal measure on the trifling and the valuable. During the last four years of her life she ceaselessly begged publishers and patrons for money and continually gave that same money away: it was not unusual for her to have £20 in the morning and £1 in the afternoon.[1] Her appearance ravaged, the goiter enlarged, she attended as many literary functions as possible, wearing large bows and scarves at her throat and home-made dresses twenty years out of fashion, eager for whatever faint praise or acknowledgment she might receive, yet highly self-conscious, finding snubs and slights in the gestures of all who attended.[2] Her old paranoia returned; once again she feared she was being poisoned.[3] Continuing to commute between Lyth Hill and London, she could achieve no peaceful resolution for her anxieties over her husband's lessening attention and her fear of his unfaithfulness. And, in fact, she now had obvious and real reason to worry. Henry's infatuation with his tutorial student, Kathleen Wilson, was abundantly clear. He rarely came home for dinner, preferring to dine with the Wilson family—hardly surprising in light of the tea, toast, and scraping that Mary Webb wrote to a friend was all they had to eat. In 1926, Henry insisted on bringing Kathleen with him when he and Mary returned to Lyth Hill for the summer. It is easy to conjecture the sorts of comparisons Webb might have made between herself, now forty-five, and Kathleen Wilson, fresh and vital at nineteen. Kathleen left after a short time and Henry and Mary began to argue. Then Henry left too. Coming back from a walk, Mary found the cottage empty of her husband and all his belongings; he had left no note telling her of his return to London. Webb was hysterical until she learned of his whereabouts.[4]

When Alice Meredith died in the spring of 1924, Mary Webb had expected some share of her mother's considerable fortune. Instead, all the money and property were given to Olive, who, still unmarried, had lived with her mother in Chester. Only Alice Meredith's jewelry was to be equally divided among the three daughters. Webb was devastated: she had expected money and, as eldest daughter, she had hoped to have first choice of her mother's jewels. As she explained to her brother, Kenneth, she needed the jewelry, not for herself but to sell.[5] Wrenn and Coles both state that Alice Meredith's death was painful for Mary emotionally, and Wrenn cites as evidence of Webb's love for her mother a poem written in 1920.[6] Both conjecture that Webb's distress at her mother's death was real and greatly intensified by her memory of her father's death fifteen years earlier. This may be the case, certainly. Yet it seems telling that Kenneth Meredith's memories of the funeral concern his sister's anger over property and money: she had actually run out of the Meredith house at one point and gone to the station to board a train for London. Webb may have experienced genuine grief, but it was overlaid with financial concern. Alice Meredith had cheated her daughter of maternal care; Mary had performed domestic tasks her mother could not. In her death, it would seem as though Alice had cheated her daughter once again.

In addition, Webb was having difficulty arranging a suitable publication agreement for *Precious Bane. Seven for a Secret,* like her previous novels, had sold somewhat more than a thousand copies—a respectable sale at the time, but hardly a best seller. Webb finally settled on Jonathan Cape, who advanced her £100, a smaller sum than she had ever before received. Webb's first two novels were now out of print, a fact which did more than depress her—it terrified her. Her literary immortality was being threatened, and, unlike Gillian Lovekin, this was not a sacrifice Webb could permit for any reason. But Cape remained adamant in his refusal to issue a cheap edition of *The Golden Arrow,* and he steadfastly refused Webb further advances on *Precious Bane,* despite pleading and sometimes accusing letters. On completing *Precious Bane,* she decided to concentrate on writing short stories, articles, and book reviews since they could be produced quickly and would bring in immediate money. Her output was considerable. Between the fall of 1923 and the spring of 1927, she wrote a total of twenty-eight reviews for the *Bookman,* the *Spectator,* and *T. P.'s and Cassell's Weekly.* Rarely did she review a single novel or simply compare two. Most often her reviews covered six or eight books at a time and were carefully crafted essays in form and content. Her writing is highly polished and intensely introspective, concerned not only with the merits of a particular author or book but with their implications for modern fiction or the role of nature in the growth of a personal aesthetic. She also spent considerable time and energy on two lengthy, carefully researched articles on historical Shropshire, later published in the Field Club *Transactions* and the *Shrewsbury Chronicle,* and she wrote approximately a dozen short stories. But despite the advance on the novel, despite the money she made reviewing, despite Henry's salary, in September of 1924 Webb wrote Jonathan Cape a letter pleading for work reading manuscripts, detailing her poverty: "I pay cash for food [so] these sudden bills mean that I starve. My husband has his chief meals out (at school), but I don't."[7]

Webb's ravaged appearance and her frenetic pace were symptoms of her failing health. She had severe pains in her neck and head and dizzy spells, which often caused her to faint.[8] At Alice Meredith's funeral, the family had been shocked by Webb's physical deterioration: she looked like a woman of sixty.[9] According to Wrenn, in early 1924 Henry had become concerned with his wife's dizzy falls and insisted that she see a doctor, the same one who had "cured" her when she had been ill before their wedding. The doctor now informed Henry of the nature and extent of his wife's illness— Graves' disease plus pernicious anemia. Henry left the doctor, aware that Mary had at most four years before her disease would ultimately cause her death.[10] Coles does not mention such a visit, nor suggest that Henry Webb was aware of what Mary was not: that she was dying. But if Henry did know his wife's diagnosis, then his continued infatuation with Kathleen Wilson seems insensitive if not cruel. Wrenn, either because certain letters and interviews were not available to her, or because, like the earlier biographers, she would prefer to present a positive picture of the Webb marriage, interprets Henry's actions as the product of wisdom (he knew that he needed to be alone), necessity (he needed to be in London for his work), and exhaustion (he was truly worn out with the constant demands and reproaches of the last three years). And Wrenn dismisses, as well, Henry's interest in Kathleen Wilson as no more than a mentor's benevolent interest in a bright student. Coles is the sole biographer to depict Henry in a less than sympathetic light: Henry did not bring Kathleen to Lyth Hill in the last year of his wife's life because, as Wrenn postulates, he thought the girl's youth and energy would cheer his wife and end her brooding. The truth was that Henry was fascinated with Kathleen and could not bear to be parted from her.[11]

The point here is not recrimination; life with Mary Webb could only have been difficult. What is of importance is that in a life which she perceived as marked by the loss of the security and love her father had provided—a loss she attempted to fill with her husband and her work—Webb appeared to lose again. Her husband was gone; her mother had cheated her; her novels were going out of print. She was neither the happy wife and mother she forced her own characters to become, nor was she the famous and applauded author she would not let them be. She had never become her mother, nor had she triumphed over her. Neither had she regained her father. And if Henry had been George's replacement, she now saw him moving away from her as well. Life must have seemed an endless act of subtraction.

Henry's unannounced departure from Lyth Hill that summer did not result in their final separation and the end of their marriage, as Webb feared. Henry had sought advice from his headmaster and friend, Joseph Wicksteed, who suggested legal separation and apparently wrote to Mary about the matter. But when she returned to London, Henry informed her that he intended to stay with her, and they continued their marriage. Nonetheless, circumstances were strained, and Henry was distant both emotionally and physically, spending even more time at school or tutoring Kathleen Wilson.[12] Mary's health grew worse; she slept little and could hardly write. The only cheer in her life at this time was a letter from Stanley Baldwin, the prime minister, praising *Precious Bane*. Webb was overjoyed to receive his letter, and pleased that the novel was selling well, yet at this time she also wrote to a friend that she now felt that there was "little left to live for."[13]

In the summer of 1927, Mary Webb returned to Lyth Hill alone, so weak that she could walk only slowly and then not far. She forced herself to write a review for the *Bookman*—of Edith Wharton's *Twilight Sleep,* which failed for her because "there is no inevitability, there is nothing of the sense of helpless humanity struggling in a net set for it before time was."[14] When she returned to London in the fall, she found Henry unchanged and unresponsive. With her she had brought the partial manuscript of a new novel that she had been unable to work on, *Armour Wherein He Trusted*. The novel was probably begun as early as 1925, but Webb found herself unable to make headway on it. Written in the first person, it had a narrator who seems to be no more than an attenuated masculine version of *Precious Bane*'s Prue Sarn set in a medieval context. The theme is repetitive of *Gone to Earth* and *Seven for a Secret:* the clash between carnal and spiritual love. The lyricism of *Precious Bane,* which makes even some of the more precious language lovely, is nowhere to be found in this last novel, embarrassing in its use of archaic diction. In September 1927, Webb attempted to destroy the manuscript. Too weak to tear it, though she initially tried, she threw it into the fire. For better or worse, Henry rescued it; Coles conjectures that she felt relief that it had been saved, but I am not so certain.[15]

In February 1926, Mary Webb received the Prix Femina Vie Heureuse for *Precious Bane*.[16] The resultant publicity was good for sales, and the novel went into a fourth printing.[17] On October 8, 1927, she died in a coma. She had wanted to be near Minoni, her childhood governess, and so had journeyed to a nursing home in Sussex, near Minoni's home in West Hill, St. Leonard's-on-Sea. Even before her arrival, she collapsed and had to be carried from the train to the taxi that would take her to Quarry Hill Nursing Home. Henry arrived shortly after her death; Coles terms him inconsolable.[18] She was brought home to Shropshire and buried in Shrewsbury cemetery, near Meole Brace on 12 October. Six months later Stanley Baldwin publicly acclaimed her novels before a large literary gathering; the next day newspapers gave prominence to his tribute, although they had hardly noted Webb's death. She became an overnight sensation, and Henry became a very wealthy man on the royalties. Two years later, Henry married Kathleen Wilson; in 1939, he fell to his death while walking in the Lake District, and Kathleen, left with their two young children, inherited the estates of both Henry and Mary Webb. Four years later, Kathleen married Jonathan Cape, Mary Webb's last publisher, who purchased from his wife the Webb copyrights. Like Mary, Kathleen Cape died at the early age of forty-six.

Precious Bane, her most acclaimed book, as of 1985 had gone through more than fifty printings and nine editions, as well as a dramatized version presented in 1931 and a television drama in the 1960s. [19] As with all Webb's novels, critical evaluation is scanty. One of the novel's characters supplied Britain's prospective parents with a name that was faddish for a time—Jancis—but reviewers wrote the same tired appreciations of Webb, an appreciation now enhanced by the fact that "the little rustic" was dead and had lived nearly unknown, unappreciated, unheard. The irony lies in the fact that her success created—and endured on—an image of her which obscured the truth rather than presented it. Webb was famous not for herself but for what her reviewers and biographers wanted her to be—the homespun mystic of the Shropshire hills. She was presented not as complicated and tortured, but as simple and suffering. The real Webb now dead bore small resemblance to the unreal Webb now living.

Of the critical appraisals of *Precious Bane,* one stands out—Barbara Hannah's. [20] A Jungian analyst, Hannah interprets the novel as Webb's attempt at integration of the disparate and warring parts of her own personality. Hannah's criticism is frequently marred by her tendency to consider the novel's characters as real individuals, possessing real psyches and histories, but her criticism still remains the single piece of in-depth evaluation of any Webb novel. Of the other critics who discuss *Precious Bane*—Gladys Coles, and Glen Cavaliero are in Hannah's debt. Hannah views *Precious Bane* as Webb's attempt to accept a world of evil as well as good, and herself as capable of both bad and good action. It is an attempt characterized by the novel's very title, an oxymoron that suggests the possibility of a junction between what is valuable and what is poisonous, between what is holy and what is murderous. The novel fails, according to Hannah, because Webb is ultimately unable to accept the presence of evil in the world, and so allows good to triumph in a world that contains neither the dark nor doubtful. [21] What a literary critic might term a contrived ending in which the evil are properly punished and the good rewarded, Hannah considers a conclusion that is brought about through a psychic failure of courage: Webb could not face evil; she could only banish it. Thus Hannah views Webb's final novel as indication of her inability to accept the hidden horrors of her inner self, and views that personal failure as cause of a critical failure.[22]

Hannah's insight into *Precious Bane*'s failure is especially interesting in light of what she did not know when she wrote her criticism: Webb wrote the last chapter of *Precious Bane* first, and then created a novel to lead to that happy end. But while Hannah considers the novel proof of its author's psychic defeat by her inner forces, the novel also gives evidence of Webb's final attempt to deal with her maternal history, and it is an attempt that succeeds, at least partially: Webb kills a mother even as she allows that mother to provide a daughter with a loving surrogate in the form of a husband. In other words, the mother gives her daughter a gentle and tender husband, but the mother is murdered by the daughter's subverted complicity. Hannah considers this murder of the mother, which occurs through the daughter's negligence, proof that the novel's author-daughter is unable to meet the demands of her psyche for integration and wholeness because she cannot allow into consciousness her knowledge that this murder is going to happen. Nor can she, after the murder has taken place, admit her responsibility for its occurrence.[23] However, the fact that the mother is good but nonetheless killed is evidence that Webb remained unable to completely resolve the author-daughter's ultimate conflict: how does she both accept the maternal and reject it at the same time? How does she become wife while not emulating the mother but becoming the individual self—the writer?

The novel, despite its critical acclaim and broad popularity, does fail, as Hannah suggests, in terms of enabling the author to achieve "psychic resolution." Webb still cannot find the proper locus of blame for the daughter's dichotomous desire. She still cannot determine who is at fault for the daughter's dual need to separate from—even reject—the mother while still seeking her love. Nor can Webb name the agent responsible for the pain and evil she sees in the world around her, an agent unnamed but nonetheless demonstrated in this novel, as in her others, to be a patriarchally dominated society. By the novel's conclusion, it is clear that she will lay the blame for suffering on the sufferer, just as she has before. Hannah identifies Webb's thinking as an example of the Thomistic theory of *privato boni,* which denies evil separate, real existence. According to Hannah, in Webb's convoluted metaphysics evil becomes no more than a matter of interpretation. Could the sufferer properly view her circumstances, she would find not pain, but simply the absence of pleasure, just as winter is no more than the absence of summer. Suffering, thus, is self-caused because it is merely a matter of personal interpretation rather than the product of nature or society or family.

Webb is considerably more sophisticated than purveyors of "look-on-the-bright-side" philosophy; she does not merely attempt to ignore the presence of pain and evil. Rather she denies their very existence. If the victim is made responsible for her own agony, then the world of external forces cannot be blamed. On the one hand, this makes the victim guilty as well as suffering. On the other hand, it gives the individual control. External forces that cause pain cannot be controlled, but interpretations can be. The sufferer is not powerless but is empowered to change that which she cannot endure. Such a view of evil's nonexistence deflects anger, sublimates it. An impotent rage, which once focused on an external world it could neither bend to its will nor escape, can now be directed against the sufferer. Thus even while Webb canonizes her victims she makes them suffer still further. She loves Rwth but has her murdered; she loves Hazel but has her killed. Webb believed in and used the power of language to state the truth, but she closed her own mouth and starved herself to death.

The self-reflexiveness of evil and blame Webb posits is mirrored most particularly in *Precious Bane.* Anger once thrust on the external world is deflected and ultimately embedded in the self. The landscape of *Precious Bane* takes on the contours of the psyche; the characters do not move out into the world but are confined in ever tighter, ever more smothering environments. As with all her novels, *Precious Bane* opens with a lengthy description of the landscape, in this case the house and lands of the Sarn family. The setting is completely enclosed, nearly claustrophobic. The house is placed within a valley; within that valley is yet a further depression, Sarn Mere, the small pool where Prue Sarn often goes. The mere is utterly placid and reflects what visually surrounds it—trees and vegetation and the sky above—as well as the sounds which fill the still country air, such as church bells. Sky and trees tower over the small human inhabitants, and all are reflected and echoed in the surface of the mere once again. There is only this landscape and its unvarying reflection, making the world of Sarn and of *Precious Bane* nearly solipsistic, a Celtic knot in which beginning and end—cause of pain and bearer of pain—cannot be disentangled. While Webb's other novels pay careful attention to and give much description of the natural landscape, in no other novel is that landscape quite so cloistering. The grotto of *The House in Dormer Forest* is certainly terrifying and imprisoning, but it is not the only landscape of the novel. Amber does not walk only there, but also walks through woods and forests offering comfort rather than threat. The natural world of *Precious Bane,* though never once actually termed enclosing or described as threatening, is forbidding by the fact of its seamlessness, its imprisonment.

Within this world, we are told the story of the Sarn family, the mother and father—one kind but weak and the other brutal—and of Gideon, the oldest son, and his sister, Prue, the novel's narrator, who has a harelip. In *The Golden Arrow, Seven for a Secret,* and *Gone to Earth,* the major conflict of the story concerned the heroine's need to choose the "right" kind of love: spiritual rather than carnal. In *The House in Dormer Forest,* Amber herself was never in doubt as to the correctness of her decision to love Michael Hallowes, but in the other female characters of the novel Webb demonstrated the terrible results of love perverted for mere sexuality or power. In *Precious Bane,* Prue Sarn loves immediately and correctly a man who returns her love despite her physical deformity. Prue's brother, Gideon, whose struggle to choose love over wealth reiterates the theme of all Webb's novels, ultimately fails. He sends away the woman he loves, Jancis, and their child with her. She drowns herself and her child, and Gideon, haunted by her death, follows her into the mere. Free from her brother and her promise to him to work on the farm until they are rich, Prue leaves Sarn, meets with Kester the Weaver, the man she loves, and they marry. The novel is narrated by Prue as an old woman, happy though childless, in an attempt to set down "the whole truth" so as to blot out any lies that might still be told about her story.

With her "hare-shotten" lip, Prue Sarn is related to several of Webb's earlier female characters who bear a physical mark of some sort: Gillian Lovekin with the "Devil's mark" upon her forehead, the mark disappearing when she finally, sobbingly acquiesces to Robert's mastery; Amber Darke whose poor complexion contrasts with her sister's bloom and Catherine's lovely paleness; Hazel Woodus whose blood-spattered clothing and hands foretell her own brutal end. Nor can Webb's own appearance be ignored; at the time *Precious Bane* was written, Webb's disfigurement from Graves' disease was most obvious.[24] But Prue displays important differences from these earlier characters. She is neither adolescently callow like Gillian, nor innocently ignorant like Hazel. Prue is strong and practical, and, unlike the passive Amber, she uses her own physical strength and bravery to save Kester Woodseaves' life and thereby ensure his love. Thus while Prue's harelip links her with Webb's earlier heroines, Prue is distinctly not a copy of any one of them.

Prue's harelip is ultimately responsible for her triumph in the world of Sarn. Her deformity is her "precious bane." Because she is marred, Prue's life does not follow the usual pattern of the women around her; she cannot, therefore, be expected to replicate her mother's life. Prue had always expected to marry and have children. When Gideon exacts her promise to work for him "as a servant, for no money, until all that he will be done,"[25] he does so by pointing out that no one will ask her to wed. Prue is stunned; although she had always heard her mother moan, "Could I help it if the hare crossed my path?" she had never been conscious of the true meaning of that curse and its mark. It is a mark that the country folk believe to be a sign of a witch but a sign that for Prue means the denial of all her hopes.[26] Prue agrees to labor as "a prentice, a wife, and a dog" for her brother since he promises her, in turn, a house and furniture, china and gowns, if she will help him.[27] He promises as well that he will give her money to send away for a cure. Yet after Prue swears her oath to Gideon and he to her, she feels "as if Sarn Mere was flowing right over us, and I shivered as if I'd got an ague."[28] This is, contends Hannah, a sign whose significance Webb allows her character to ignore.

Prue's marred appearance denies her the usual life of wife and motherhood she had always expected to lead. Her deformity and its consequences now apparent to her, Prue is impelled to do Gideon's bidding, though she suspects that it is a dark bidding as she gazes into her brother's cold eyes. But she agrees because while Gideon cannot offer her a husband and family, he can at least assure her that she will own her own house—that she will be mistress of her space. Gideon cannot promise her that she will have happiness, but he can promise her that she will have the power that material possessions and adequate money ensure.

Gideon inherited the farm on his father's sudden death. That death, occurring in the midst of his towering rage, calls for the services of a Sin Eater—one who will take upon himself the sins of the deceased by eating his bread and drinking his measure of wine—if the deceased is not to walk at night but rest in peace. But the stingy Gideon is unwilling to spend money for such services. Instead, at the burial, when the minister calls out to ask if a Sin Eater is present, Gideon uses his mother's distress to blackmail her: he will be the Sin Eater if she will deed him the farm immediately. She unhappily agrees, and Gideon takes up "the little pewter measure full of darkness" and the bread and eats and drinks.[29] The farm becomes Gideon's, and Gideon becomes Sarn rather than young Sarn. Gideon is unconcerned that his neighbors consider him cursed for having taken upon himself the sins of another man.

Prue gives up her desire for the feminine life she had ex-

pected and joins her fate with that of her brother, whose actions stem from his greed for money as well as from the
darker strains of human desire. Neither Prue's prophetic
shiver after her vow, nor Webb's description of Gideon's Sin
Eating leaves any doubt that Prue's allegiance to Gideon's plan
is wrong and that nothing good can come from it. But once
again the oxymoron of the novel's title applies. Because Prue
works for her penny-pinching brother, she is taught to read
and write. And because she can read and write, Prue can woo,
via letters, Kester Woodseaves, the weaver. Thus, while
Prue's decision and Gideon's desires may be dark and even
evil, for Prue, at least, they lead to love. That such good can
derive from so terrible a source—that love can come from
greed and the lust for power—may well simply underscore
the *privato boni* principle which Hannah contends shapes the
novel. But another interpretation is also possible.

Previous chapters have demonstrated that Webb used her
female characters and their relationship to their mothers, to
power, and to society, as a means of resolving the predica-
ment faced by a daughter who became an author rather than
a mother. In her first novel Webb created sympathetic and
maternal Patty Arden whom Deborah could emulate. But
Webb also provided a mentor-father who was Deborah's
most powerful model. It is he who enables her to accept human love as less than perfect. Deborah learns domestic tasks
from her mother; she learns to love, however, from her father. In *Gone to Earth,* Hazel Woodus only poorly matures
because of the neglect of her father and the deprivation of
strong and good maternal figures. Hazel is free to make herself, but she is unable to love because she has no model for
"safe" love—a love that allows union as well as autonomy.
No one, mother, father, husband, lover, or even surrogate
mother, is able to demonstrate the means by which one can
give up freedom, take up the demands of marriage and maternity, and yet be happy. Gillian Lovekin, too, grows up
without a mother and is guarded, but hardly guided, by her
loud and none-too-clever father. Because she is loved by the
mystical Robert, a character much like John Arden, Gillian

finally does give up her desires for fame and wealth and immortality. She learns to accept the biological immortality of children instead. Amber Darke and Michael Hallowes are well-matched lovers. Each is equally capable of passionate as well as spiritual love. Despite her cold and even sadistic mother and her ineffectual father, Amber is easily able to sacrifice all for love—even leaving the woods and going to some distant city if that is what Michael demands as a test of her love.

All of these women end by denying their original demands, even Hazel, who dies because she cannot make that denial in time to live. All of these characters, in other words, ultimately emulate their mothers. With the exception of Amber, all become mothers. Each of these characters chooses *not* to fulfill a role that is other than her mother's. Each character chooses *not* to fulfill her own desires, and instead decides to renounce her need for individuality through her choice to lose herself as wife. Although Webb was very eager for fame herself, although she was intensely unhappy following her husband from Shropshire to London, although she hardly fulfilled the role of housekeeper and did not fulfill that of mother, Webb created four novels about women who gave up precisely what she would not, and chose exactly what she could not.

In her fifth novel, however, Webb created Prue Sarn, who gives up her hopes of marriage in order to gain power, and who then uses the power in order to win love. Prue may be marred, and she may have made a pact with a not very disguised devil, but she will be given the immense power of the written word, and with that power she will win her own happiness. Because of her deformity, Prue differs from other women; but it is this deformity that offers her salvation. The story of *Precious Bane* can be read as an allegory of the authoring woman whose needs and talents set her apart, label her as "witch" and as "unnatural," ally her with the world of men and power rather than home and hearth, but who finds in her literary "curse" the means by which she can alleviate her own unhappiness.

Prue is aware of the power that her writing confers. She knows that it provides her with a hold over her illiterate brother. If he treats her poorly, she can find herself suddenly unsure of the alphabet and thus unable to write his letters for him. Her literacy is a power she can use should Gideon not treat their mother well. Writing gives her the status to demand decent treatment for herself and for her mother, for another woman who lacks all power of self-protection. In addition, Prue's book-learning has begun to fill some of the lonely spaces in her rather solitary life.

Prue's appearance and her vow to her brother have isolated her. Prue and her mother are presented as fairly gregarious; they know their neighbors, and they talk with them. But with her vow to her brother, Prue leaves the kitchen and begins to work like a man. There is little of the farm work that she does not and cannot perform, Gideon remarks with pride. She labors from morning until dark, often at tasks for which men on neighboring farms would hire extra help. Since Gideon begrudges her money for cloth, Prue wears ragged clothing and goes hatless and shoeless most of the year. Working hard and speaking little, Prue is left with time for thought. She finds that her learning has begun to fill her mind with thoughts that grow "like flowering rushes and forget-me-nots coming into blow in a poor marshy place, that else had nought."[30] The inner self is born.

Prue's place of refuge is the attic. There she can open the shutter which looks out on the orchard and smell the scent of wild roses and hear the birds:

I harkened to the blackbirds singing near and far. When they were a long way off you could scarcely disentangle the thrushes and willow-wrens, seven-coloured linnets, canbottlins, finches, and *writing-maisters*. It was a weaving of many threads, with one maister-thread of clear gold, a very comfortable thing to hear.[31]

This is what she thinks love must be like, a tapestry of many colored threads with one of clear gold—the master thread. Prue is able to have what no other female character achieved.

She has a sure sense of love as the master thread, but she understands it also as one of *many* strands in the tapestry of her life, *and* she has a definite place which is her own, where she can be herself, satisfy her literary and mystical longings. Prue can be "at peace" with her need for love and union because she has the privacy of her attic where she can feel and express herself. Unlike Gillian Lovekin, Prue can both love and be fully herself.

In the attic Prue has an experience which changes her life. The experience can only be described as mystical since she undergoes a sense of transcendence like that of religion's union with Godhead:

It was as if some creature made all of light had come on a sudden from a great way off, and nestled in my bosom. On all things there came a fair, lovely look, as if a different air stood over them. It is a look that seems ready to come sometimes on those gleamy mornings after rain, when they say, "so fair the day, the cuckoo is going to heaven."[32]

The feeling is one that seems to come and go for the rest of her life and is identified forever with the attic. It is a sense of there being "a core of sweetness in much bitter," and enables her to endure the privations of her life. As she learns to read and write, Prue takes her ink and quill and ledger to the attic and hides them in an old locker. She writes surrounded by the hundreds of apples stored for the winter:

I fell to thinking how all this blessedness of the attic come through me being curst. For if I hadna had a harelip to frighten me away into my own lonesome soul, this would never have come to me. The apples would have crowded all in vain to see a marvel, for I should never have known the glory that came from the other side of silence.

Even while I was thinking this, out of nowhere suddenly came that lovely thing, and nestled in my heart, like a seed from the core of love.[33]

Thus her harelip has set her apart, but the boon of this difference is that she has gained something beyond the usual. Like

Rwth, Prue knows what lies beyond the bounds of language. But unlike Rwth, she did not need to die to learn this mystery.

★　★　★

Prue is taught to write by Master Beguildy, the local magician and the father of Jancis, whom he has forbidden to marry Gideon. Beguildy is without scruples. It is not that Beguildy thinks that Gideon does not love his daughter but rather that Beguildy hopes to "sell" her to a local squire of some wealth. He makes Jancis pose at night in their cottage window, a lamp glowing behind her and making her yellow hair seem gold; he has posed her there in hopes of a "buyer." Beguildy's magic is fake, and his wife and daughter, and soon Prue, see his magical power for what it is: a lazy way of earning money, of forcing his wife to contend with the physical labor of the farm, and of soothing his ever-damaged ego. Nonetheless, Beguildy is quick to realize Prue's intelligence, and he is a good teacher. While there is something amusing in the character of Beguildy, there is also something sordid in his lying and drunkenness and self-adulation. He is nothing more than a clever form of Gideon. Both men value money over love; both men are willing to use Jancis for their own mercenary ends; both men are quite willing to let women labor to death.

Beguildy has promised young Squire Camperdine that with the proper words and magic—and the proper amount of money—the goddess Venus can be raised. He intends to perform this feat by rigging up a pulley and ropes and creating a chemical smoke screen into which Jancis will be raised, naked, from a trapdoor between the cellar and parlor. Jancis has refused to carry out her father's wishes because she fears that Gideon may find out that she has appeared naked to another man. Prue offers to perform in Jancis's place, saving her from a beating from her father as well as from Gideon's possible knowledge. Prue plans to veil her head in muslin so that her face will not reveal to Beguildy that "Venus" has been switched.

When Prue is hoisted into the dimly lit room she discovers,

to her utter horror, that Kester Woodseaves is there as well as the squire. Having met Kester once, when he came to do weaving for Jancis's future wedding, Prue has fallen in love with him. But she has decided that she must hide herself from him forever, lest he see her face and feel pity for her. Now, as she stands naked before him, she realizes that he desires her:

It came upon me then with great joy that it was my own self and no other that had made him hold out his arms. For in that place he could not see my curse, he could only see me gleaming pale as any woman would.[34]

Prue is now aware for the first time that although her face is marred, her body "was as passable as any woman could be."[35] She is happy that she has given her body in this way to "the eyes of him who was maister in the house of me for ever and ever."[36]

* * *

The scene is certainly a curious one, and bears no resemblance to any scene in Webb's other novels. The novel's critics have taken the scene at face value: it is a moment when Prue realizes that she is sexually attractive, and it is an opportunity for Kester himself to fall utterly in love with her. But there is something more here, as well. The magical act of raising Venus is a sham, of course, a fiction. Beguildy performs the act for the payment he receives; the squire wants to see the act not because he is under any illusion as to the magical powers of Beguildy but because he wants to see a naked woman. (Indeed, as he leaves he is still trying to get the name of the "Venus" so that he might have further—and, one assumes, more intimate—dealings with her.) From such crass desire comes, once again, something quite beautiful and profound. From fiction comes the truth: Prue is beautiful and desirable. Within the fictive act there is the possibility for revelation of the self. In a novel dealing with a woman who comes to power through her writing, this strange scene of wizards and hoists and a naked woman suggests much about Webb's perception of her own writing. When revealed in her art, she is unmarred, whole and beautiful.

Further use of the fictive as a means for arriving at truth is present in Prue's circuitous wooing of Kester. Jancis has been hired out to a dairy farmer some distance away. Gideon has Prue write letters to Jancis for him. Since Jancis cannot read, she goes to the weaver to have the letters read. Kester is aware of the fact that Prue writes the letters for her brother. As he reads each letter to Jancis he reads words clearly and obviously meant for him: Gideon's love letter to Jancis is, in fact, Prue's love letter to Kester. Prue's ability to write enables her to gain the love and the husband she had thought lost to her. It is her power rather than the abnegation of self that wins Prue her heart's desire.

★   ★   ★

As in none of her previous novels, Webb creates in *Precious Bane* a mother who, though sickly and fearful, can nonetheless aid her daughter in choosing and winning the right lover. Mrs. Sarn cannot protect Prue from Gideon's near-forced labor, but she does enable her daughter to succeed in love. Prue and Gideon go to Lullingford's fair where a bull-baiting is about to begin. Kester is horrified and attempts to halt the affair by offering to singlehandedly tie each dog to its chain, claiming that because he has made friends with all these animals in the past they will not harm him. There is, however, a new dog in town, and this dog proves to give him trouble. Prue watches the weaver for a moment and then runs to find, first a large carving knife, and then the apothecary whom she brings to the ring. When she arrives, the dog has grabbed Kester by the throat, and he has fainted. Prue stabs the dog and orders the apothecary to burn the bite clean. The weaver recovers from his faint, and Prue, in turn, swoons. When she awakens, Kester has been taken away. Prue's mother realizes that her usually shy daughter would never have performed so publicly, much less so dangerously, did she not love the weaver. Mrs. Sarn decides to spin night and day, producing so much yarn that Gideon must call in the weaver. When Prue carries out her earlier promise not to meet the weaver face to face and so leaves for the day, Mrs. Sarn uses the opportunity to praise her daughter to Kester, and finally persuades him to admit that should he ever consider marriage it would be to a woman like Prue. That night, when Prue returns, her mother implores her to no longer hide from Kester. In fact, her mother encourages Prue to pursue him aggressively.

While Mrs. Sarn is timid and easily terrified, first by her husband and now by Gideon, she remains a source of support and advice for her daughter. In turn, Prue protects her mother against Gideon's bullying and attempts to find work for her mother that is not heavy and difficult. But after the ready-to-be-harvested field has been set afire by Beguildy— the field which had promised enough money for Gideon to finally wed Jancis—Gideon's insistence that his mother is a burden becomes constant. Prue listens and says nothing as night after night Gideon tries to make his mother admit that she would be better off dead. When the old woman finally agrees, Gideon ends his nightly visits to his mother. Sometime later, Gideon has a conversation with the doctor about the poisonous qualities of foxglove tea, which, since it contains digitalis, is very dangerous for the old lady, who has heart trouble. When Gideon poisons his mother with the tea, the doctor is naturally suspicious, but he can prove nothing.

Barbara Hannah finds Prue's seemingly willful ignorance of her mother's murder the product of Prue's displacement of all her energy and interest into Kester and love. Prue, she suggests, has only one goal in life and so ignores all that does not help her in its attainment. She is aware that Gideon has killed her mother, but she closes her conscious mind to what her unconscious mind knows very well.[37] Although she does not herself administer the fatal tea, she has been given every hint that Gideon wants his mother dead. When her mother dies and the doctor is suspicious, she has every clue as to what has occurred, but she is silent.

Hannah is clearly suggesting that Webb created a character who is willfully blind to the cause of her mother's death because Webb herself preferred to remain blind to the nature and existence of evil in the world. Webb would prefer to explain the dark as nothing more than the absence of light. But her denial of evil as real has already been apparent in her other novels where that denial functions, as it does here, to absolve patriarchal power as the source of pain, frustration, loss of self. It is Beguildy who burns Gideon's fields, thereby making Gideon's marriage to Jancis impossible. It is Gideon who plans to use the foxglove tea, manipulating the infatuated—and pregnant—parson's daughter, Tivvy, into its actual administration. It is a male standard of female beauty that naive Prue finally accepts and so enters into her bond with Gideon. While some of these evils end in good, Jancis, her child, and Gideon nonetheless drown, unredeemed by love, and Mrs. Sarn is murdered.

Mrs. Sarn is not the only mother to die in this novel. Jancis, whom Gideon has slept with but then refused to marry because of Beguildy's arson, returns to Sarn with their child. Gideon is unmoved by the sight of either Jancis or the half-starved baby. He mocks both and rejects them. Tivvy, who is in love with Gideon and terrified that Jancis might win him back, threatens to reveal that Gideon gave his mother the foxglove tea. Prue is so horrified at the possibility of this revelation that she pays no attention to Jancis and her baby. Thus Jancis is able to creep off from the house and drown herself and her child in the mere. Hannah suggests that, once again, there were sufficient clues and warnings for Prue to suspect that Jancis had suicide in mind.[38] But Webb, and hence Prue, preferred blindness.

Hannah does not suggest that Prue willfully desires the death of her mother, nor that Webb did. She sees both instances as evidence for her theory that Prue has aligned herself with Gideon's dark animus and so must ignore, and even destroy, the creativity of the individual. Hannah suggests that not only does Prue allow her own feminine creativity to be destroyed, but that she also allows the font of creativity—the maternal body—and the seeds of life—Jancis's child—to be destroyed. Hannah sees the character of Tivvy—ugly, stupid, petty, and herself pregnant by Gideon—as the shadow, or dark half, of Prue's psyche. Tivvy knows what Prue ignores, and Tivvy acts.[39]

Tivvy as Prue's psychic shadow is an interpretation that

works well in light of Hannah's Jungian criticism. And Hannah's suggestion that Prue's blindness to her mother's murder and Jancis's suicide is most puzzling does seem correct.[40] Webb, however, does not seem to consider Prue culpable in any way. Webb permits Prue to be aware of the events, but does not allow Prue to prevent them, to feel guilty remorse that she cannot stop them, nor even to hate the brother who has caused these deaths to occur. If Tivvy is Prue's dark shadow, then Prue is Webb's. Perhaps Webb allows Prue to permit tacitly the murder of Mrs. Sarn and Jancis's suicide because she would have a character perform what the author could not consciously desire.

Mrs. Sarn has given Prue aid in gaining the love of Kester. It was her mother who "cursed" her with the physical deformity, yet who helps her find the love she needs for happiness. But when this mother becomes a burden she is killed. It would have been awkward, had Mrs. Sarn not died, for Webb to remove Prue from the farm after Gideon's death. While the farm and animals can be disposed of, some arrangements would need to be made for an invalid mother. In terms of the plot, in other words, it was necessary to remove Mrs. Sarn from the story. But there were other ways for Mrs. Sarn to die, other ways to remove her. Webb chose murder, and she chose to write that murder in such a way that Prue must have some awareness of it. The mother is killed, and Prue is innocent. Prue is not only not guilty, but, perhaps equally important, Prue feels no guilt.

It is Tivvy who ultimately accuses Prue. After Gideon has drowned himself in the mere, Prue takes the animals to the fair to sell them. Tivvy, who now hates Prue for having slapped her and insulted her when she was attempting to keep Jancis and her child away from Gideon, takes her revenge by declaring to the townspeople that Prue has murdered her mother and has prevented Gideon's marriage to herself. Always suspicious that Prue's harelip is a sign that she is a witch, the townspeople tie Prue to the ducking stool and proceed to lower her into the water. Kester, however, comes on the scene, fights off the crowd, and saves Prue. As the two ride off into the coming evening, Kester bends his head and kisses Prue "full upon the mouth."[41]

The ending is hardly a surprise. We have certainly been prepared for a uniting of Prue and Kester; we have known from the beginning that the townspeople believe Prue is a witch; we have watched Tivvy's jealousy and rage grow. As with her previous novels, *Precious Bane*'s ending is dramatically romantic, the lovers posed on a horse placed against an evening sunset. But what does not happen in this novel is the love scene in which the woman agrees to give up all. Although Prue insists again and again that the weaver is her master, that he is her godlike savior, that he is the single gold thread—the master thread—in the tapestry of her life, she undergoes no change for him, makes no sacrifice of self. Prue gets what she always wanted, and she is largely responsible for obtaining it: she saved Kester from death; she wrote the letters that charmed him. And after their marriage, as she makes clear in the novel's beginning, she continues to write.

In this final novel, Webb created the woman who both benefits from and vanquishes her mother. She created the woman who works like a man, learns the magician's power of writing, gains a lover and husband through her strength rather than her weakness, marries, has no children, and is happy still, many years later, when she writes in order to tell the truth about herself. If *Precious Bane* is Webb's best novel—and it is—perhaps it is because it is the novel in which she finally expressed her deepest desires. In her four earlier novels Webb punished women who wanted too much. She killed women who would not sacrifice. In her last novel Webb had to kill a mother in order for a daughter to separate from her, but she finally allowed a daughter to grow. And she enabled that daughter to achieve both love and autonomy—union and selfhood—as well as the literary power to tell the story of that achievement.

Conclusion

A New Perspective

> Who is there when a woman says, "I am"?
> JUDITH KEGAN GARDINER, *"On Female Identity"*

Gladys Coles and Dorothy Wrenn conclude their biographies of Mary Webb by noting the irony of her own obscure and hardly noticed death followed by her novels' immediate emergence into literary fame, and her husband's sudden wealth.[1] Coles points out the growth of a number of Mary Webb Societies in Britain and America,[2] and discusses the parodic handling of rural themes and country lives in Stella Gibbons' *Cold Comfort Farm,* defending Webb against the generally held belief that Gibbons based her 1932 satire directly on Webb's novels.[3] Both authors praise Webb's poetic and "mythic" sensibilities, to some extent deflecting emphasis on Webb's psychic complexities or her novels' critical problems. Coles, in particular, while suggesting that it is time to reassess Webb with "fresher eyes," suggests that as a writer Webb cannot easily be classified; in order to reevaluate Webb we must "set aside the conventional frames of reference, the usual tenets of criticism."[4] Webb is too much the mystic to fit simple definition, rigid categorization.

Still, if Webb's work is to be considered as having significance, then it must be allowed to take its place within the critical arena. And within that arena, Webb offers valuable insight into the nature of women's literary creativity. This is not to suggest that Webb is a major, undiscovered writer whose radical revision of the fictive process was ignored because of her gender. In fact, as her publication history makes clear, Webb was being read, reprinted, and reviewed—on two continents—two decades after her death. But because even these later reviews indicate that she continued to be admired for her depictions of the rural and the charm of her romances, Coles is correct in her claim that reassessment is necessary. Feminist criticism offers a stance from which Webb's work as texts within a context can be illuminated. We can come to some understanding of *this* woman and *her* fictive re-creation of the world, and we can come to further understanding of women writers' imaginative manipulation of fact into fiction.

But this is not to deny that Webb presents a number of difficulties for the feminist critic. During the last decade, when feminist criticism developed and burgeoned, the works most often given attention were those which had the surface appearance of "feminism" or which could be read as "code"—as telling feminist tales in secret, as filled with covert rebellion. Yet Mary Webb's life gives only small indication of "feminist sympathies," and her work is filled with deflected insights into the nature of women's conflicts, women's oppression. She would be the last to suggest that the complexities of her history and psyche were the result of her gender or of patriarchy. While *The House in Dormer Forest* and *Gone to Earth* contain explicit criticism of the terrible lives endured by those women and men who accept their social roles and shape their lives to fit the patterns created by others, and while she clearly abhors the false convention of sexual modesty decreed for both men and women, Webb nonetheless chose not to examine closely the structure which created such roles, values, and conventions. Placing blame instead on the individuals who succumbed to external expectations, she absolved her society. But even as she maintained the power of the individual to break from convention and achieve her desires, she proceeded to punish those female characters who did so.

Meek rather than rebellious, Webb wrote novels which suggest over and over again that among her greatest afflictions was the fact of her childlessness, and that among her greatest joys was her role as self-sacrificing wife. Living in an age in which British rural life was undergoing enormous change, she chose not to admit such change into the world of her novels. She created green countrysides in which industrialism, war, and even modern methods of dairy farming had no part. Birth control is an issue in *The Golden Arrow,* but not a possibility. Yet in none of her novels are cottage wives overburdened with a dozen children, nor is death during childbirth ever mentioned.

What evaluation, then, is the feminist critic to render when considering Mary Webb? Or, to put this question into different terms, what does the study of Mary Webb add to our understanding of the nature of women's writing? Because authorship is an act of power whereby the individual creates the world she desires, an examination of Webb's novels expands our understanding of the world women would create. Since writing is an act of power, those women who write, whether covertly or overtly rebellious, perform an action clearly in opposition to their society's expectations. And in so doing, the woman writer—even one who denies independence to the creatures of her own imagination—asserts her ability to create what she would have. As an individual Webb starved herself, but as an author she found the means for her satisfaction. That the authorial self does not match the personal self seems sad but not inexplicable. Such warring self-division is the expected lot of those who accept their lack of right to have the very things they most desire.

Despite the ambivalencies and griefs of Mary Webb's life, and despite the frequency with which they mar her writing, as a woman writer she deserves critical appraisal rather than elegiac sentiment. Webb's writing may display self-pity or self-devaluation, but her essays, her aggressive self-selling of her novels and reviews, her desire to enter into London's literary establishment, her overwhelming need for fame, give reason to readjust the earlier "rustic rhetoric" that characterizes her critics' evaluation. She did take to her sickbed early in life and return there with suspicious frequency when her life was not to her liking. But she also repeatedly left her bed and resumed writing at a furious pace. She could recline pas-

couch, but she also walked vigorously into the countryside, and wrote about doing so. Even as she seemed intent upon dying, she wrote a novel in which a strong female character found a way to achieve her own happiness. Having struggled unsuccessfully throughout her life with her need to placate or reject her mother, she wrote a novel in which the heroine is both accessory to and blind to the murder of her mother. Thus, like all writers, her life is not entirely mirrored in her work. There she is different—both stronger and weaker. And like all writers, her work necessarily mirrors mind and desire. She denied what she would have and sought it nonetheless. She refused what she wanted even as she gave that wanting creative life and literary breath. Arguing for romantic love's supremacy, she still desired fame and immortality; she is, most simply and most complexly, a woman who wrote.

Notes

Introduction

1. D. H. Lawrence, *Lady Chatterley's Lover* (New York; Grove Press, Inc., 1959 reprint of 1928 edition), p. 212.

2. Edward Said, "Molestation and Authority in Narrative Fiction," in *Aspects of Narrative.* ed. J. Hillis Miller (New York; London: Columbia University Press, 1971), pp. 47–68.

3. Helene Moglen, *Charlotte Bronte: The Self-Conceived* (New York: W. W. Norton & Company, Inc., 1976), p. 84.

4. Tania Modleski, *Loving with a Vengeance* (New York; London: Methuen, 1982), pp. 28–31.

5. Phyllis Chesler, *Women and Madness* (Garden City, N.Y.: Doubleday, 1972), See in particular the Introduction and Chapter Three.

6. Adrienne Rich, "Splittings," in *Dream of a Common Language* (New York: W. W. Norton & Company, Inc., 1978), p. 11.

Chapter 1: Author as Daughter

1. Carroll Smith-Rosenberg, "The Female World of Love and Ritual: Relations between Women in Nineteenth-Century America," *Women's Experience in America,* eds. Esther Katz and Anita Rapone (New Brunswick: Transition Books, 1980), pp. 259–92.

2. Margaret Homans, *Women Writers and Poetic Identity* (Princeton: Princeton Univ. Press, 1980), p. 14.

3. Carol Dyhouse, *Girls Growing Up in Late Victorian and Edwardian England* (London: Routledge and Kegan Paul, 1981), p. 31.

4. Elaine Showalter, "Florence Nightingale's Feminist Complaint," *Signs,* 6, No. 3 (1981), 401.

5. Judith Pildes, "Mothers and Daughters," *Frontiers: A Journal of Women Studies,* 3, No. 2 (1978), p. 1.

6. Gladys Mary Coles, *The Flower of Light* (London, Gerald Duckworth, 1978), p. 25.

7. Barbara Hannah, "Mary Webb," *Striving Towards Wholeness* (London: Allen and Unwin, 1972), pp. 72–104; Hilda Addison, *Mary Webb* (London:

Cecil Palmer, 1931); Thomas Moult, *Mary Webb* (London: Jonathan Cape, 1932, and Dorothy P. H. Wrenn, *Goodbye to Morning* (Shrewsbury: Wilding, 1964).

8. Wrenn, p. 107.

9. W. Reid Chappell, *The Shropshire of Mary Webb* (London: Cecil Palmer, 1930).

10. W. Byford-Jones, *Shropshire Haunts of Mary Webb* (Shrewsbury: Wilding, 1948).

11. Coles, p. 9.

12. Coles, pp. 9–11.

13. Coles, p. 21.

14. Moult, p. 16.

15. Flora Thompson, *Lark Rise to Candleford* (London: Oxford University Press, 1945), pp. 148–66.

16. As quoted in Phyllis Stock, *Better than Rubies* (New York: Putnam, 1978), p. 177.

17. Dyhouse, p. 44.

18. Dyhouse, p. 44.

19. Dyhouse, p. 45.

20. Coles, pp. 33–34.

21. Coles, p. 50; Wrenn, p. 22; Moult, pp. 55–56.

22. Ellen Moers, *Literary Women* (Garden City: Anchor Books, 1977), p. 198.

23. Simone de Beauvoir, *The Second Sex* (New York: Knopf, 1957), pp. 363–64.

24. Elaine Showalter, *A Literature of Their Own* (Princeton: Princeton Univ. Press, 1977).

25. Sandra M. Gilbert and Susan Gubar, *The Madwoman in the Attic* (New Haven: Yale University Press, 1979), pp. 248–308.

26. Wrenn, pp. 13–18.

27. Wrenn, p. 23; Coles, pp. 41–42.

28. Wrenn, pp. 13, 17–18; Coles, p. 31.

29. Wrenn, p. 30.

30. Wrenn, p. 30.

31. Wrenn, p. 31.

32. Wrenn, pp. 51–53.

33. Carroll Smith-Rosenberg, "The Hysterical Woman: Sex Roles and Role Conflict in Nineteenth-Century America," *Women's Experience in America,* p. 316.

34. Smith-Rosenberg, "The Hysterical Woman," p. 316. See also Gilbert and Gubar, *The Madwoman in the Attic,* pp. 57–59.

35. Juliet Mitchell, *Women: The Longest Revolution* (New York: Pantheon, 1984) pp. 287–94.

36. Mitchell, *Women,* pp. 289–90.

37. Mitchell, *Women,* p. 290.

38. Coles, p. 238.

39. Wrenn, p. 36.

40. Wrenn, p. 36.

41. Mary Webb, *Poems and The Spring of Joy* (London: Jonathan Cape, 1948), p. 128.

42. Webb, *Poems,* pp. 149–50.

43. Webb, *Poems,* p. 215.

44. Edith Holden, *Country Diary of an Edwardian Lady* (Exeter: Webb & Bower, 1977); reprint, Holt, Rinehart and Winston.

45. Webb, *Poems,* p. 127.

46. Wrenn, p. 39.

47. Webb, *Poems,* p. 86.

48. Wrenn, p. 44.

49. Coles, pp. 98–103; Wrenn, pp. 44–45.

50. Wrenn, p. 48; Coles, pp. 107–08, who gives the gardener's surname as Downes rather than Dowsett.

51. Wrenn, pp. 49–50.

52. Wrenn, p. 48.

53. Coles, p. 106.

54. Wrenn, pp. 40–41.

Chapter 2: The Golden Arrow

1. Mary Webb, *The Golden Arrow* (London: Jonathan Cape, 1945).

2. Dorothy P. H. Wrenn, *Goodbye to Morning* (Shrewsbury: Wilding and Sons, 1964), p. 52.

3. Wrenn, p. 52.

4. See Raymond Williams, *The Country and The City* (New York: Oxford University Press, 1973), pp. 255–58. See also Glen Cavaliero, *The Rural Tradition in the English Novel, 1900–1939 (Totowa, N.J.: Rowman and Littlefield, 1977)* and W. J. Keith, *The Rural Tradition* (Toronto: University of Toronto Press, 1974).

5. The novel was received with favorable if scanty reviews, a fact, suggests Wrenn, that had more to do with the war than with Webb's novel itself (Wrenn, p. 58).

6. For a discussion of the novel's presentation of love see Charles Sanders, "*The Golden Arrow:* Mary Webb's

'Apocalypse of Love,'" *English Literature in Transition*, No. 10 (1967), pp. 1–8.

7. Webb, *The Golden Arrow*, p. 253.

8. Webb, *The Golden Arrow*, pp. 255–56.

9. Webb, *The Golden Arrow*, p. 256.

10. Webb, *The Golden Arrow*, p. 253.

11. Webb, *The Golden Arrow*, p. 256.

12. Webb, *The Golden Arrow*, pp. 82–83.

13. Webb, *The Golden Arrow*, p. 75.

14. Glen Cavaliero, pp. 145–46.

15. Webb, *The Golden Arrow*, p. 37.

16. Webb, *The Golden Arrow*, p. 23.

17. Webb, *The Golden Arrow*, p. 14.

18. Webb, *The Golden Arrow*, p. 14.

19. Webb, *The Golden Arrow*, p. 71.

20. Webb, *The Golden Arrow*, p. 165.

21. Webb, *The Golden Arrow*, p. 167.

22. Webb, *The Golden Arrow*, p. 176.

23. Webb, *The Golden Arrow*, p. 177.

24. Webb, *The Golden Arrow*, p. 177.

25. Webb, *The Golden Arrow*, p. 177.

26. Webb, *The Golden Arrow*, pp. 177–78.

27. Webb, *The Golden Arrow*, p. 163.

28. Webb, *The Golden Arrow*, p. 144.

29. Webb, *Poems and The Spring of Joy* (London: Jonathan Cape, 1948), p. 71.

Chapter 3: Gone to Earth

1. Gladys Mary Coles, *The Flower of Light* (London: Gerald Duckworth, 1978), p. 158.

2. Dorothy P. H. Wrenn, *Goodbye to Morning* (Shrewsbury: Wilding, 1964), pp. 58–59.

3. Coles, p. 152.

4. Coles, p. 155.

5. Wrenn, p. 63.

6. Coles, p. 155.

7. Coles, pp. 155–57.

8. Wrenn, p. 60.

9. Coles, p. 159.

10. Coles, p. 155.

11. John Buchan in *Gone to Earth* (London: Jonathan Cape, 1932), p. 1 of an unnumbered Introduction.

12. Mary Webb, *Gone to Earth* (London: Jonathan Cape, 1932), p. 105.

13. Wrenn, pp. 8–9; Moult, p. 31.

14. Wrenn, p. 61.

15. Webb, *Gone to Earth*, p. 12.

16. Susan Peck MacDonald, "Jane Austen and the Tradition of the Absent Mother," *The Lost Tradition*, eds. Cathy N. Davidson and E. M. Broner (New York: Frederick Ungar, 1980), p. 58.

17. Webb, *Gone to Earth*, p. 20.

18. Webb, *Gone to Earth*, p. 28.

19. Webb, *Gone to Earth*, p. 28.

20. Webb, *Gone to Earth*, p. 28.

21. Webb, *Gone to Earth*, p. 29.

22. Webb, *Gone to Earth*, p. 29.

23. Webb, *Gone to Earth*, pp. 29–30.

24. In this description of Undern Hall as charnel house, one is reminded of Poe's House of Usher. But literary influence is difficult to demonstrate here and, in fact, does not increase insight into this novel.

25. Webb, *Gone to Earth*, p. 193.

26. Webb, *Gone to Earth*, p. 44.

27. Webb, *Gone to Earth*, p. 47.

28. Webb, *Gone to Earth*, p. 49.

29. Webb, *Gone to Earth*, p. 50.

30. Webb, *Gone to Earth*, p. 50.

31. Webb, *Gone to Earth*, p. 71.

32. Webb, *Gone to Earth*, p. 62.

33. Webb, *Gone to Earth*, pp. 13, 19.

34. Webb, *Gone to Earth*, p. 135.

35. Webb, *Gone to Earth*, p. 103.

36. Webb, *Gone to Earth*, p. 107.

37. Webb, *Gone to Earth*, p. 106.

38. Webb, *Gone to Earth*, pp. 91–92.

39. Webb, *Gone to Earth*, p. 159.

40. Webb, *Gone to Earth*, p. 146.

41. Webb, *Gone to Earth*, p. 147.

42. Webb, *Gone to Earth*, p. 147.

43. Webb, *Gone to Earth*, p. 151.

44. Webb, *Gone to Earth*, p. 175.

45. Webb, *Gone to Earth*, p. 177.

46. Webb, *Gone to Earth*, p. 179.

47. Webb, *Gone to Earth*, p. 178.

48. Webb, *Gone to Earth*, p. 189.

49. Webb, *Gone to Earth*, p. 192.

50. Webb, *Gone to Earth*, p. 193.

51. Webb, *Gone to Earth*, p. 215.

52. Webb, *Gone to Earth*, p. 217.

53. Webb, *Gone to Earth*, p. 233.

54. Webb, *Gone to Earth*, p. 256.

55. Webb, *Gone to Earth*, p. 263.

56. Webb, *Gone to Earth*, p. 265.

57. Webb, *Gone to Earth*, p. 287.

58. Webb, *Gone to Earth*, p. 288.

59. Webb, *Gone to Earth*, p. 205.

60. Webb, *Gone to Earth*, p. 53.

61. Webb, *Gone to Earth*, p. 53.

Chapter 4: The House in Dormer Forest

1. Thomas Moult, *Mary Webb* (London: Jonathan Cape, 1932), pp. 186–87; Gladys Mary Coles, *The Flower of Light* (London: Gerald Duckworth, 1978), p. 180.

2. Dorothy Wrenn, *Goodbye to Morning* (Shrewsbury: Wilding, 1964), pp. 65–70.

3. Wrenn, pp. 70–71; Coles, pp. 199–200.

4. Wrenn, pp. 71–73; Coles, pp. 200–01.

5. Wrenn, pp. 71–73.

6. Wrenn, p. 71.

7. Wrenn, pp. 71–72.

8. Wrenn, p. 73.

9. Coles, p. 182.

10. Wrenn, pp. 70–71.

11. Wrenn, p. 72.

12. Coles, p. 202.

13. Wrenn, pp. 72–75.

14. Coles, p. 212.

15. Wrenn, p. 75.

16. Wrenn, p. 75.

17. Moult, p. 176.

18. Susan Peck MacDonald, "Jane Austen and the Tradition of the Absent Mother," *The Lost Tradition*, eds. Cathy N. Davidson and E. M. Broner (New York: Frederick Ungar, 1980), pp. 58–69.

19. Mary Webb, *The House in Dormer Forest* (London: Hutchinson, 1920), p. 10.

20. Webb, *The House in Dormer Forest*, p. 10.

21. Webb, *The House in Dormer Forest*, p. 10.

22. Webb, *The House in Dormer Forest*, p. 11.

23. Webb, *The House in Dormer Forest*, p. 11.

24. Webb, *The House in Dormer Forest*, p. 12.

25. Webb, *The House in Dormer Forest*, p. 12.

26. Moult, p. 169; Glen Cavaliero, *The Rural Tradition in the English Novel, 1900–1939* (Totowa, N.J.: Rowman and Littlefield, 1977), p. 139.

27. Wrenn, p. 67.

28. Coles, pp. 186–192.

29. Coles, p. 186.

30. Cavaliero, p. 139; Wrenn, p. 67.

31. Coles, p. 188; Wrenn, p. 68.

32. Coles, pp. 189–90.

33. Webb, *The House in Dormer Forest,* p. 172.

34. Webb, *The House in Dormer Forest,* p. 172.

35. Webb, *The House in Dormer Forest,* p. 173.

36. Webb, *The House in Dormer Forest,* p. 173.

37. Webb, *The House in Dormer Forest,* p. 174.

38. Webb, *The House in Dormer Forest,* p. 153.

39. Webb, *The House in Dormer Forest,* pp. 153–54.

40. For a discussion of the relationship between literary landscapes, female topography, and women writers, see Ellen Moers, *Literary Women* (New York: Anchor Books, 1977), pp. 382–89.

41. Webb, *The House in Dormer Forest,* p. 172.

42. Webb, *The House in Dormer Forest,* p. 154.

43. Webb, *The House in Dormer Forest,* pp. 153–61.

44. Webb, *The House in Dormer Forest,* p. 290.

45. Webb, *The House in Dormer Forest,* p. 27.

46. For a somewhat dated and highly flowery discussion of Webb's mysticism and its connection to sexuality, see Margaret Lawrence, *The School of Femininity* (New York: Frederick A. Stokes, 1936), pp. 331–38.

47. Webb, *The House in Dormer Forest,* p. 134.

48. Webb, *The House in Dormer Forest,* p. 15.

49. Webb, *The House in Dormer Forest,* p. 15.

50. Webb, *The House in Dormer Forest,* p. 134.

51. Webb, *The House in Dormer Forest,* p. 14.

52. Webb, *The House in Dormer Forest,* p. 21.

53. Webb, *The House in Dormer Forest,* p. 133.

54. Webb, *The House in Dormer Forest,* pp. 280–81.

Chapter 5: Seven for a Secret

1. Dorothy Wrenn, *Goodbye to Morning* (Shrewsbury: Wilding, 1964), p. 64.

2. Gladys Mary Coles, *The Flower of Light* (London: Gerald Duckworth, 1978), p. 235.

3. Coles, pp. 219–21.

4. Coles, p. 237.

5. Coles, p. 246.

6. Coles, p. 237.

7. Coles, p. 238.

8. Coles, p. 224.

9. Coles, p. 240.

10. Barbara Hannah, "Mary Webb," *Striving Towards Wholeness* (London: Allen and Unwin, 1972), p. 73.

11. Coles, pp. 241–43.

12. Coles, pp. 228–29.

13. Coles, p. 229.

14. Glen Cavaliero, *The Rural Tradition in the English Novel, 1900–1939* (Totowa, N.J.: Rowman and Littlefield, 1977), p. 141.

15. Wrenn, p. 82.

16. Coles, p. 228.

17. Cavaliero, p. 141.

18. Wrenn, p. 82.

19. Margaret Lawrence, *The School of Femininity* (New York: Frederick A. Stokes, 1936), p. 337. Lawrence views Webb as portraying men as biologically "free" since they are not "doomed to bear the burden of life," while women love men "yearningly and wistfully" precisely because they are not doomed as women are. Because of woman's love for man, she "reconciles herself to her lot."

20. For an excellent analysis of the romance as pornography and pornography's use of female submission see Ann Barr Snitow, "Mass Market Romance: Pornography for Women Is Different" and Jessica Benjamin, "Master and Slave: The Fantasy of Erotic Domination" in *Powers of Desire: The Politics of Sexuality*, eds. Ann Snitow, Christine Stansel, and Sharon Thompson (New York: Monthly Review Press, 1983), pp. 245–63, 280–99. I have purposely refrained from using the term pornography in direct reference to *Seven for a Secret*. I have done so not simply because the novel lacks explicit sexual detail—Rwth's rape and her beatings are relayed to us in retrospect and without specifics—but because as a term pornography is so laden with explosive connotation that its application here would change the direction in which I intend to take this discussion of Webb's novel. That male domination of a woman, whether physical or psychological or emotional, is "pornographic" is the subject of an argument other than the one I make here. But that women's romantic tales describe a socially acceptable form of male domination and female submission is a premise I accept as a given.

21. Steven Marcus, *The Other Victorians* (New York: Basic Books, 1974), pp. 211–12.

22. Webb, *Seven for a Secret* (New York: E. P. Dutton, 1929), p. 84.

23. Webb, *Seven for a Secret*, p. 24.

24. Webb, *Seven for a Secret*, p. 212.

25. Webb, *Seven for a Secret*, p. 296.

26. Webb, *Seven for a Secret*, p. 242.

27. Webb, *Seven for a Secret*, pp. 242–43.

28. Webb, *Seven for a Secret*, p. 271.

29. Webb, *Seven for a Secret*, p. 267.

30. Webb, *Seven for a Secret*, p. 268.

31. Webb, *Seven for a Secret*, p. 271.

32. Webb, *Seven for a Secret*, p. 273.

33. Webb, *Seven for a Secret*, p. 274.

34. Webb, *Seven for a Secret*, p. 275.

Chapter 6: Precious Bane

1. Gladys Mary Coles, *The Flower of Light* (London: Gerald Duckworth, 1978), p. 277.

2. Coles, pp. 282–83.

3. Dorothy P. H. Wrenn, *Goodbye to Morning* (Shrewsbury: Wilding, 1964), p. 95.

4. Coles, pp. 300–01.

5. Coles, pp. 277–78.

6. Wrenn, pp. 93–94.

7. Coles, p. 277.

8. Wrenn, p. 85; Coles, p. 279.

9. Wrenn, p. 93.

10. Wrenn, pp. 85–86.

11. Wrenn, pp. 95–96; Coles, pp. 300–01.

12. Coles, pp. 301–02.

13. Coles, p. 303.

14. Mary Webb, "Irony and Mrs. Wharton," originally published in *The Bookman*, Sept. 1927, p. 303, and available in *Collected Prose and Poems,* ed. Gladys Mary Coles (Shrewsbury: Wilding, 1977), pp. 69–70.

15. Coles, p. 314.

16. In 1928 Virginia Woolf received the same prize for *To the Lighthouse*.

17. Coles, p. 300.

18. Coles, p. 317.

19. Coles, p. 324; Wrenn, pp. 106–07.

20. Barbara Hannah, "Mary Webb," *Striving Towards Wholeness* (London: Allen and Unwin, 1972), pp. 72–104.

21. Hannah, p. 77.

22. Hannah, p. 103.

23. Hannah, pp. 93–98.

24. Coles, p. 279.

25. Mary Webb, *Precious Bane* (London: Jonathan Cape, 1931), p. 42.

26. Webb, *Precious Bane*, p. 20.

27. Webb, *Precious Bane*, p. 42.

28. Webb, *Precious Bane*, p. 43.

29. Webb, *Precious Bane*, pp. 35–36.

30. Webb, *Precious Bane*, p. 68.

31. Webb, *Precious Bane*, p. 58.

32. Webb, *Precious Bane*, p. 58.

33. Webb, *Precious Bane*, p. 60.

34. Webb, *Precious Bane*, pp. 115–16.

35. Webb, *Precious Bane*, p. 116.

36. Webb, *Precious Bane*, p. 117.

37. Hannah, pp. 95–96.

38. Hannah, pp. 96–97.

39. Hannah, p. 95.

40. Hannah, p. 94.

41. Webb, *Precious Bane*, p. 288.

Conclusion

1. Gladys Coles, *The Flower of Light* (London: Gerald Duckworth, 1979), pp. 323–25; Dorothy Wrenn, *Goodbye to Morning* (Shrewsbury: Wilding, 1964), pp. 105–06.

2. Coles, p. 327.

3. Coles, pp. 326–27.

4. Coles, p. 330.

Bibliography

Books by Mary Webb (dates of first editions)

The Golden Arrow. London: Constable, 1916.
The Spring of Joy. London: J. M. Dent, 1917.
Gone to Earth. London: Constable, 1917.
The House in Dormer Forest. London: Hutchinson, 1920.
Seven for a Secret. London: Hutchinson, 1922.
Precious Bane. London: Jonathan Cape, 1924.
Armour Wherein He Trusted: A Novel and Some Stories. London: Jonathan
  Cape, 1929.
Poems and The Spring of Joy. London: Jonathan Cape, 1928.
The Chinese Lion. London: Rota, 1937.
Fifty-One Poems. London: Jonathan Cape, 1946.
A Mary Webb Anthology. Ed. Henry B. L. Webb. London: Jonathan Cape,
  1939.
The Essential Mary Webb. Ed. Martin Armstrong. London: Jonathan Cape,
  1949.
Mary Webb: Collected Poems and Prose. Ed. with intro. Gladys Mary Coles.
  Shrewsbury: Wilding, 1977.
Mary Webb: Selected Poems. Ed. with intro. Gladys Mary Coles. Mersey-
  side: Headland Publications, 1981.

Reviews of Books by Mary Webb

1916

"New Novels." Rev. of *The Golden Arrow*. *Times Literary Supplement* (London), 7 Sept. 1916, p. 428.

1917

"Amid the Hills of Wales." Rev. of *The Golden Arrow*. *Independent*, 2 June
  1917, p. 438.
"Among the 'Localists.'" Rev. of *Gone to Earth*. *Nation*, 105 (20 Sept.
  1917), 317.
Berenberg, D. P. "*Gone to Earth*." *New York Call*, 9 Sept. 1917, p. 15.
"*The Golden Arrow*." *New York Times Book Review*, 6 May 1917, p. 183.
"*Gone to Earth*." *Times Literary Supplement* (London), 30 Aug. 1917, p.
  416.
"*Gone to Earth*." *New York Times Book Review*, 26 Aug. 1917, p. 318.
"List of New Books." Rev. of *Gone to Earth*. *Athenaeum*, No. 4621 (Sept.
  1917), 471.

"Notes on New Fiction." Rev. of *The Golden Arrow. Dial,* 62 (7 May 1917), 443–44.

"Notes of New Fiction." Rev. of *Gone to Earth. Dial,* 63 (13 Sept. 1917), 220.

1920

"Novels in Brief." Rev. of *The House in Dormer Forest. Athenaeum,* No. 4710 (6 Aug. 1920), p. 179.

"New Novels." Rev. of *The House in Dormer Forest. Times Literary Supplement* (London), 22 July 1920, p. 471.

"*The House in Dormer Forest.*" *London Mercury,* 11 (Sept. 1920), 626–27.

1921

Hopkins, Mary Alden. "Family Fetishes." Rev. of *The House in Dormer Forest. Publisher's Weekly,* 99 (19 Feb. 1921), 574.

"*The House in Dormer Forest.*" *New York Times,* 30 Jan. 1921, p. 23.

Mann, D. L. "*The House in Dormer Forest.*" *Boston Evening Transcript,* 26 Jan. 1921, p. 8.

"New Novels." Rev. of *The House in Dormer Forest. Outlook* (London), 128 (4 May 1921), 28.

"Rebels." Rev. of *The House in Dormer Forest. Nation,* 112 (25 May 1921), 749, 791–92.

1922

Gould, Gerald. "New Fiction." Rev. of *Seven for a Secret. Saturday Review* (London), 134 (2 Dec. 1922), 843–44.

Haycraft, Howard. "The Heart of the Country." Rev. of *Seven for a Secret. Spectator,* 129 (11 Nov. 1922), 666.

"New Novels." Rev. of *Seven for a Secret. Times Literary Supplement* (London), 9 Nov. 1922, p. 726.

1923

"Books in Brief." Rev. of *Seven for a Secret. Nation,* 67 (10 Oct. 1923), 410.

Boynton, H. W. "*Seven for a Secret.*" *Independent,* 60 (23 June 1923), 406.

Gilkes, Lilian. "Rural Romance." Rev. of *Seven for a Secret. Book News and Reviews (New York Tribune),* 22 July 1923, p. 23.

H. H. "*Seven for a Secret.*" *Literary Digest International Book Review,* 1 (Sept. 1923), 59–60.

M., D. L. "*Seven for a Secret.*" *Boston Evening Transcript,* 3 July 1923, p. 6.

Mortimer, Raymond. "New Novels." Rev. of *Seven for a Secret. New Statesman,* 20 (27 Jan. 1923), 485.

Osborn, E. W. "His Life Points the Way of Life to Young Rideout." Rev. of *Seven for a Secret. New York World,* 27 May 1923, p. 6E.

Singleton, J. K. "New Novels." Rev. of *Seven for a Secret. New Republic,* 30 (27 June 1923), 129.

"A Slender Welsh Story." Rev. of *Seven for a Secret. Springfield* (Mass.) *Republican,* 22 July 1923, p. 7A.

"*Seven for a Secret.*" *New York Times,* 20 May 1923, p. 19.

"*Seven for a Secret.*" *Literary Review* (*New York Evening Post*), 20 Oct. 1923, p. 165.

1924

Clarke, Austin. "Novels." Rev. of *Precious Bane*. *Nation and Athenaeum*, 35 (2 Aug. 1924), 560–70.

Franklin, John. "New Novels." Rev. of *Precious Bane*. *New Statesman*, 23 (30 Aug. 1924), 599.

Gould, Gerald. "New Fiction." Rev. of *Precious Bane*. *Saturday Review* (London), 138 (30 Aug. 1924), 221.

Hartley, L. P. "Sacred and Profane Love." Rev. of *Precious Bane*. *Spectator*, 138 (2 Aug. 1924), 168.

"New Novels." Rev. of *Precious Bane*. *Times Literary Supplement* (London), 17 July 1924, p. 448.

1926

C., J. W. "*Precious Bane.*" *New York World,* 6 June 1926, p. 4.

Cook, S. L. "*Precious Bane.*" *Boston Transcript,* 5 June 1926, p. 5.

Field, L. M. "*Precious Bane.*" *Literary Review* (*New York Evening Post*) 29 May 1926, p. 3.

J., E. M. "*Precious Bane.*" *Springfield* (Mass.) *Republican,* 26 Sept. 1926, p. 7.

Kolars, Mary. "A Shropshire Tragedy." Rev. of *Precious Bane*. *Books* (*New York Herald Tribune*), 6 June 1926, p. 12.

Moore, L. "*Precious Bane.*" *Literary Digest International Book Review,* 26 Aug. 1926, p. 548.

"The New Books." Rev. of *Precious Bane*. *Outlook* (London), 143 (28 July 1926), 449.

"*Precious Bane.*" *Saturday Review of Literature* (New York), 11 (17 July 1926), 939.

"*Precious Bane.*" *New York Times,* 20 June 1926, p. 8.

Vaillant, Maria. "*Precious Bane.*" *Atlantic Monthly,* 138 (Sept. 1926), 22, 24.

1928

"News and Views of Literary London." *New York Times Book Review,* 20 May 1928, p. 10.

"The Poems of Mary Webb." Rev. of *Poems and The Spring of Joy*. *Times Literary Supplement* (London), 27 Dec. 1928, p. 102.

Welby, T. Earle. "Reviews: Mr. Pound and Others." Rev. of *Poems and The Spring of Joy*. *Saturday Review* (London), 146 (22 Dec. 1928), 851–52.

1929

"*Armour Wherein He Trusted.*" *Bookman* (New York), 69 (29 May 1929), 23.

"*Armour Wherein He Trusted.*" *New York Times,* 28 April 1929, p. 6.

F. B. "Mary Webb's Poems." Rev. of *Poems and The Spring of Joy*. *Boston Transcript,* 27 April 1929, p. 5.

Bogan, Louise. "Mary Webb." Rev. of *The House in Dormer Forest, Seven for a Secret,* and *Poems and The Spring of Joy. New Republic,* 59 (14 Aug. 1929), 348.

Brooks, Walter R. "Picked at Random." Rev. of *Armour Wherein He Trusted. Outlook* (London), 60 (17 April 1929), 629, 636.

Diamant, Gertrude. "*Armour Wherein He Trusted.*" *New York World,* 28 April 1929, p. 10.

Divine, Charles. "Sweet Music." Rev. of *Poems and The Spring of Joy. Books* (*New York Herald Tribune*), 14 July 1929, p. 17.

Field, L. M. "*Armour Wherein He Trusted.*" *New York Evening Post,* 13 April 1929, p. 10.

Gibson, Wilfred. "The Poems of Mary Webb." Rev. of *Poems and The Spring of Joy. Bookman* (London), 75 (Feb. 1929), 269–70.

Hawkins, Ethel Wallace. "The Books of Mary Webb." *Atlantic Monthly,* 144 (Aug. 1929), 12, 14.

K., C. M. "*Armour Wherein He Trusted.*" *Springfield* (Mass.) *Republican,* 5 May 1929, p. 7.

K., C. M. "*Poems and The Spring of Joy.*" *Springfield* (Mass.) *Republican,* 23 June 1929, p. 7.

Marshall, H. P. "Mary Webb." Rev. of Webb's *Collected Works. Edinburgh Review,* 249 (April 1929), 315–27.

"Mary Webb's Last Story." Rev. of *Armour Wherein He Trusted. Times* (London), 28 Jan. 1929, p. 17.

"New Novels." Rev. of *Armour Wherein He Trusted. Times Literary Supplement* (London), 31 Jan. 1929, p. 8.

Parsons, Alice Beal. "Mary Webb's Last Book." Rev. of *Armour Wherein He Trusted. Books* (*New York Herald Tribune*), 21 April 1929, p. 4.

"Shropshire Moods." Rev. of *Collected Works,* E. P. Dutton. *Outlook and Independent,* 152 (26 June 1929), 348.

Tasker, J. Dana. "*Poems and The Spring of Joy.*" *Nation,* 129 (24 July 1929), 96.

1931

Bellessort, André. "Littérature Etrangère." Rev. of *Precious Bane. Le Correspondant,* 322, or New Series 286 (10 Jan. 1931), 129–37.

Chapman, Grace. "Mary Webb." Rev. of *Collected Works,* Jonathan Cape. *London Mercury,* 23 (Feb. 1931), 364–71.

1932

Bellessort, André. "Littérature Etrangère: Un Roman de Mary Webb et Quelques Autres." Rev. of *The House in Dormer Forest. Le Correspondant,* 328, or New Series 242 (Sept. 1932), 777–83.

1938

Weeks, Edward. "Bookshelf." Rev. of *Gone to Earth. Atlantic Monthly,* 163 (July 1938), n.p.

1939

"*A Mary Webb Anthology.*" *Times Literary Supplement* (London), 2 Dec. 1939, p. 697.

1940

A., E. V. "*A Mary Webb Anthology.*" *Forum,* 103 (June 1920), 333.

"*A Mary Webb Anthology.*" *Books* (*New York Herald Tribune*), 17 Mar. 1940, p. 26.

"Mary Webb's Writings." Rev. of *A Mary Webb Anthology. Springfield* (Mass.) *Republican,* 3 Apr. 1940, p. 8.

"A Reader's List." Rev. of *A Mary Webb Anthology. New Republic,* 102 (15 Apr. 1940), 514.

Springer, Ann. "Woman's Genius Akin to Hardy's." Rev. of *A Mary Webb Anthology. Boston Transcript,* 6 Mar. 1940, p. 1E.

Tinker, E. L. "*A Mary Webb Anthology.*" *New York Times,* 26 May 1940, p. 23.

1947

Church, Richard. "*Fifty-One Poems.*" *Spectator,* 178 (3 Jan. 1947), 22.

H., P. J. H. "*Fifty-One Poems.*" *New York Times,* 9 Nov. 1947, p. 6.

Kees, Weldon. "*Fifty-One Poems.*" *New York Times,* 9 Nov. 1947, p. 6.

MacDonald, Gerald. "*Fifty-One Poems.*" *Library Journal,* 72 (1 Dec. 1947), 1688.

1982

Craig, Patricia. "Paperbacks in Brief." Rev. of *Seven for a Secret. Times Literary Supplement* (London), 26 Nov. 1982, 1318.

Newell, Sarah. "Two Country Classics." Revs. of *Gone to Earth* and *Precious Bane. New York Times Book Review,* 24 Oct. 1982, p. 30.

Pool, Gail. "The Hunters and the Hunted." Rev. of *Gone to Earth. The Nation,* 25 Sept. 1982, 279–81.

Biographies

Addison, Hilda. *Mary Webb: A Short Study of Her Life and Work.* London: Cecil Palmer, 1931.

Byford-Jones, W. *Shropshire Haunts of Mary Webb.* Shrewsbury: Wilding, 1948.

Chappell, W. Reid. *The Shropshire of Mary Webb.* London: Cecil Palmer, 1930.

Coles, Gladys M. *The Flower of Light.* London: Gerald Duckworth, 1978.

Moult, Thomas. *Mary Webb: Her Life and Work.* London: Jonathan Cape, 1932.

Steff, Bernard. *My Dearest Acquaintance.* Ludlow: Kings Bookshop Pub., 1977.

Wrenn, Dorothy P. H. *Goodbye to Morning: A Biographical Study of Mary Webb.* Shrewsbury: Wilding, 1964.

Bibliographies

Dassie, Michelle. "Mary Webb's Contribution to *The Bookman.*" *Caliban,* No. 6 (1969), pp. 73–76.

Leclaire, Lucien. *A General Analytical Bibliography of the Regional Novelists of the British Isles: 1800–1950*. Paris: Société d'Edition, 1954, pp. 288–90.

Manly, John Matthews. *Contemporary British Literature: Bibliographies and Outlines*. New York: Harcourt, 1921, p. 170.

Sanders, Charles. "Mary Webb: An Annotated Bibliography of Writings about Her." *English Literature in Transition*, No. 9 (1966), pp. 119–36.

Secondary Sources

Adcock, Arthur St. John. *The Glory That Was Grub Street: Impressions of Contemporary Authors*. London: Sampson, Law, n.d., pp. 321–30.

Alcorn, John. *The Nature Novel from Hardy to Lawrence*. New York: Columbia Univ. Press, 1977.

Altick, Richard D. *The English Common Reader: A Social History of the Mass Reading Public, 1800–1900*. Chicago: Univ. of Chicago Press, 1957.

Baker, Earnest A. *The History of the English Novel*. Vol X. New York: Barnes and Noble, 1960.

Beauvoir, Simone de. *The Second Sex*. New York: Knopf, 1957.

Benjamin, Jessica. "Master and Slave: The Fantasy of Erotic Domination," *Powers of Desire: The Politics of Sexuality*. Eds. Ann Snitow, Christine Stansell, Sharon Thompson. New York: Monthly Review Press, 1983, pp. 280–99.

Bentley, Phyllis. *The English Regional Novel*. London: Allen and Unwin, 1941.

Blythe, Ronald. *Akenfield: Portrait of an English Village*. New York: Dell, 1973.

Brittain, Vera. *The Testament of Youth: An Autobiographical Study of the Years 1900–1925*. London: Gollancz, 1933.

Calder, Jenni. *Women and Marriage in Victorian Fiction*. London: Thames and Hudson, 1976.

Cavaliero, Glen. *The Rural Tradition in the English Novel, 1900–1939*. New Jersey: Rowman and Littlefield, 1977.

Chapman, Raymond. *The Victorian Debate: English Literature and Society, 1832–1901*. New York: Basic Books, 1968.

Chapple, J. A. V. *Documentary and Imaginative Literature, 1880–1920*. New York: Barnes & Noble, 1970.

Chesler, Phyllis. *Women and Madness*. Garden City, N.Y.: Doubleday, 1972.

Chew, Samuel C. "The Nineteenth Century and After." *A Literary History of England*. Ed. Albert C. Baugh. New York: Appleton-Century-Crofts, 1948, p. 1472.

Chodorow, Nancy. "Family Structure and Feminine Personality." *Women, Culture and Society*. Eds. Michelle Rosaldo and Louise Lamphere. Stanford: Stanford Univ. Press, 1974, pp. 43–66.

———. "Mothering, Object-Relations, and the Female Oedipal Configuration." *Feminist Studies*, 4, No. 1 (1978), 137–57.

———. *The Reproduction of Mothering: Psychoanalysis and the Sociology of Gender*. Berkeley: Univ. of California Press, 1978.

Clark, Kenneth. *Landscape into Art*. Boston: Beacon Press, 1969.

Colby, Vineta. *Yesterday's Women: Domestic Realism in the English Novel.* Princeton: Princeton Univ. Press, 1974.

Collard, Lorna. "Mary Webb." *Contemporary Review,* 143 (1933), 455–64.

Collins, Joseph. *Taking the Literary Pulse: Psychological Studies of Life and Letters.* New York: George H. Doran, 1932, pp. 207–18.

Davidson, Cathy N., and E. M. Broner, eds. *The Lost Tradition: Mothers and Daughters in Literature.* New York: Frederick Ungar, 1980.

Dyhouse, Carol. *Girls Growing Up in Late Victorian and Edwardian England.* London: Routledge and Kegan Paul, 1981.

Evans, Caradoc. "Mary Webb." *Colophon,* New Series III (1938), pp. 63–66.

Gardiner, Judith Kegan. "On Female Identity and Writing by Women." *Writing and Sexual Difference.* Ed. Elizabeth Abel. Chicago: Univ. of Chicago Press, 1982, pp. 177–91.

Gauthier, Xaviere. "Is There Such a Thing as Women's Writing?" *New French Feminists: An Anthology.* Eds. Elaine Marks and Isabelle de Courtivron. New York: Schocken Books, 1981, pp. 161–64.

Gilbert, Sandra M., and Susan Gubar. *The Madwoman in the Attic: The Woman Writer and the Nineteenth Century Literary Imagination.* New Haven and London: Yale Univ. Press, 1979.

Hannah, Barbara. "Mary Webb." *Striving Towards Wholeness.* London: Allen and Unwin, 1972, pp. 72–104.

Homans, Margaret. *Women Writers and Poetic Identity.* Princeton: Princeton Univ. Press, 1980.

Horney, Karen. "The Problem of Feminine Masochism." *Feminine Psychology.* New York: Norton, 1967, pp. 214–33.

———. "The Overvaluation of Love: A Study of a Common Present-Day Feminine Type." *Feminine Psychology.* New York: Norton, 1967, pp. 182–213.

Hynes, Samuel. *The Edwardian Turn of Mind.* Princeton: Princeton Univ. Press, 1968.

Jefferies, Richard. *Story of My Heart: My Autobiography.* New York: Macmillan, 1968.

Johnson, E. D. H., ed. *The Poetry of Earth: A Collection of English Nature Writing.* New York: Atheneum, 1966.

Jordan-Smith, Paul. *For the Love of Books: The Adventures of an Impecunious Collector.* New York: Oxford Univ. Press, 1934, pp. 76–81.

Keith, W. J. *The Rural Tradition: A Study of the Non-Fiction Prose Writers of the English Countryside.* Toronto: Univ. of Toronto Press, 1974.

Knoepflmacher, U. C., and G. B. Tennyson, eds. *Nature and the Victorian Imagination.* Berkeley: Univ. of California Press, 1977.

Lawrence, D. H. *Lady Chatterley's Lover.* New York: Grove Press, 1959 reprint of 1928 edition.

Lawrence, Margaret. *The School of Femininity.* New York: Frederick A. Stokes, 1936, pp. 331–38.

MacDonald, Susan Peck. "Jane Austen and the Tradition of the Absent Mother." *The Lost Tradition: Mothers and Daughters in Literature.* Eds. Cathy N. Davidson and E. M. Broner. New York: Frederick Ungar, 1980, pp. 58–69.

Marcus, Steven. *The Other Victorians: A Study of Sexuality and Pornography in Mid-Nineteenth-Century England*. New York: Basic Books, 1966.

Miller, Alice. *The Drama of the Gifted Child* (originally published as *The Prisoners of Childhood*). Trans. Ruth Ward. New York: Basic Books, 1981.

Mitchell, Juliet. *Psychoanalysis and Feminism*. New York: Pantheon, 1974.

———. *Women: The Longest Revolution*. New York: Pantheon, 1966.

Mitford, Mary Russell. *Our Village*. New York: Dutton, 1963 reprint.

Modleski, Tania. *Loving with a Vengeance: Mass Produced Fantasies for Women*. New York: Methuen, 1982.

Moers, Ellen. *Literary Women*. Garden City: Anchor Books, 1977.

Moglen, Helene. *Charlotte Brontë: The Self Conceived*. New York: Norton, 1976.

Newton, A. Edward. *End Papers: Literary Recreations*. Boston: Little, Brown, 1933, pp. 36–46.

Nightingale, Florence. *Cassandra*. Intro. Myra Spark. New York: The Feminist Press, 1979 reprint.

Peake, Gladys E. "The Religious Teaching of Mary Webb." *The Congregational Quarterly*, No. 11 (1933), pp. 41–51.

Pildes, Judith. "Mothers and Daughters: Understanding the Roles." *Frontiers: A Journal of Women Studies*, Vol. III, No. 2 (1978), pp. 1–11.

Pitfield, Robert L. "The Shropshire Lass and Her Goitre: Some Accounts of Mary Meredith Webb and Her Works." *Annals of Medical History*, IV (13 July 1942), 284–93.

Pugh, Edwin. "Mary Webb." *The Bookman*, July (1928), pp. 193–96.

Ramas, Maria. "Freud's Dora, Dora's Hysteria: The Negation of a Woman's Rebellion." *Feminist Studies*, Vol. 6, No. 3 (1980), 472–510.

Reed, John R. *Victorian Conventions*. Athens: Ohio Univ. Press, 1975.

Rich, Adrienne. *Dream of a Common Language*. New York: Norton, 1978.

Rigney, Barbara Hill. *Madness and Sexual Politics in the Feminist Novel*. Madison: Univ. of Wisconsin Press, 1978.

Said, Edward. *Beginnings: Intention and Method*. New York: Basic Books, 1975.

———. "Molestation and Authority in Narrative Fiction." *Aspects of Narrative: Selected Papers from the English Institute*. Ed. J. Hillis Miller. New York: Columbia Univ. Press, 1971, pp. 47–68.

Sanders, Charles. "*The Golden Arrow*: Mary Webb's 'Apocalypse of Love.'" *English Literature in Transition*, No. 10 (1967), pp. 1–8.

Showalter, Elaine. "Florence Nightingale's Feminist Complaint: Women, Religion, and Suggestions for Thought." *Signs*, 6, No. 3 (1981), 395–412.

———. *A Literature of Their Own: British Women Novelists from Bronte to Lessing*. Princeton: Princeton Univ. Press, 1977.

Smith-Rosenberg, Carroll. "The Female World of Love and Ritual: Relations Between Women in Nineteenth-Century America." *Women's Experience in America: An Historical Anthology*. Eds. Esther Katz and Anita Rapone. New Brunswick: Transaction Books, 1980, pp. 259–92.

———. "The Hysterical Woman: Sex Roles and Role Conflict in Nineteenth-Century America." *Women's Experience in America: An His-*

torical Anthology. Eds. Esther Katz and Anita Rapone. New Brunswick: Transaction Books, 1980, pp. 315–37.

Snitow, Ann Barr. "Mass Market Romance: Pornography for Women Is Different." *Powers of Desire: The Politics of Sexuality.* Eds. Ann Snitow, Christine Stansell, and Sharon Thompson. New York: Monthly Review Press, 1983, pp. 245–263.

Spacks, Patricia Meyer. *The Female Imagination.* New York: Avon Books, 1976.

Stock, Phyllis. *Better than Rubies: A History of Women's Education.* New York: G. P. Putnam's Sons, 1978.

Swinnerton, Frank. *The Georgian Scene.* New York: Farrar and Rinehart, 1934.

Thompson, Flora. *Lark Rise to Candleford: A Trilogy.* Intro. by H. J. Massingham. London, New York, Toronto: Oxford Univ. Press, 1946 reprint.

Thompson, Thea. *Edwardian Childhoods.* London, Boston, and Henley: Routledge & Kegan Paul, 1982.

Van Den Berg, J. H. "The Subject and His Landscape." *Romanticism and Consciousness: Essays in Criticism.* Ed. Harold Bloom. New York: W. W. Norton & Company, Inc., 1970, pp. 57–64.

Warner, Sylvia Townsend. *Scenes of Childhood.* New York: The Viking Press, 1982.

Westkott, Marcia. "Mothers and Daughters in the World of the Father." *Frontiers: A Journal of Women Studies.* Vol. III, No. 2 (1978), pp. 16–21.

Williams, Raymond. *The Country and the City.* New York: Oxford Univ. Press, 1975.

Zimmerman, Bonnie. "'The Mother's History' in George Eliot's Life, Literature, and Political Ideology." *The Lost Tradition: Mothers and Daughters in Literature.* Eds. Cathy N. Davidson and E. M. Broner. New York: Frederick Ungar Publishing, 1980, pp. 81–94.

Index

abortion, 50
  in *The Golden Arrow,* 42, 53–54
Addison, Hilda, 1, 5
alienation:
  alleviated by marriage, 6–7
  female happiness and, 6
allegories:
  of Webb's emerging sense of author-
    ship, 137–141
  of Webb's personality, 123–124
anatomy-destiny relationship:
  in *Gone to Earth,* 8, 87–88
  nineteenth-century notion of, 8
  in psychoanalytic models of female
    sexual development, 127
anemia:
  Webb afflicted with, 26, 120, 145
  women's ailments diagnosed as, 26–
    27
Armour Wherein He Trusted (Webb),
  142, 146–147
art-life distinction, 3–4
autonomy-domination conflict:
  female "nature" and, 126, 128
  in *The Golden Arrow,* 132, 133
  in *Gone to Earth,* 132, 133
  in literature of sexual domination,
    126, 127, 128
  love and, 125–128
  male brutalization and, 126, 128
  in *Precious Bane,* 154–155
  and rightness of female self-
    abnegation, 126–127, 128, 131–132
  in romance novels, 126, 128
  in *Seven for a Secret,* 124–128, 131–
    134, 137, 140–141
  of Webb, 124–125, 132–134, 137,
    140–141, 155
autonomy-romance conflict, 4

Baldwin, Stanley, 146, 147
beauty, feminine, 111–112
Beauvoir, Simone de, 20
Benjamin, Jessica, 118

Bennett, Arnold, 19
birth:
  dominated by males, 139
  see also maternity
birth control, 49, 50
  invalidism as form of, 26, 47, 50–51
Bodley Head, The, 35
Bookman, 119, 144, 146
Bookman Circle, 119
Browning, Elizabeth Barrett, 28
Buchan, John, 63, 64, 91
Byford-Jones, W., 16

Cambridge University, 17, 19
Cape, Jonathan, 144, 147
Cariad, 48
Cavaliero, Glen, 148
  on *The House in Dormer Forest,* 97
  on landscape of *The Golden Arrow,* 48
  on *Seven for a Secret,* 123
"Cedar Rose, The" (Webb), 35
Chappell, W. Reid, 15–16
Chaucer, Geoffrey, 9
Chester, Henry Webb's teaching post
  at, 61–62, 143
Chester, Phyllis, 10
Christianity, Webb's rejection of, 115
Cold Comfort Farm (Gibbons), 165
Coleridge, Samuel Taylor, 33
Coles, Gladys Mary, 15, 148
  on Alice Meredith's death, 143
  on Alice Meredith's invalidism, 24
  on *Gone to Earth,* 62–63
  on Henry Webb, 145, 147
  on *The House in Dormer Forest,* 97, 98
  on need for reassessment of Webb,
    165, 166
  on *Seven for a Secret,* 122–123
  on Webb's fascination with children,
    92, 93
  on Webb's illness, 94
  on Webb's philanthropy, 121
  on Webb's writing block, 119
  on Webb's writing habits, 61

About the Author

Michèle Aina Barale, a lecturer in women studies at the University of Colorado, has received two research grants—an NEH grant and a Woodrow Wilson women's studies research grant. She is a graduate of Loyola University (B.A. 1968) and of the University of Colorado (Ph.D. 1983). Barale earlier was instructor in English at Gardner-Webb College, North Carolina, and at Regis College in Denver. She is an author (with Sarah Norton and Brian Green) of *The Bare Essentials: Writing Skills*. Barale is a member of the editorial board of *Frontiers: A Journal of Women Studies*. Her home is in Boulder, Colorado.

About the Book

Daughters and Lovers was composed in Linotron 202 Bembo by Graphic Composition of Athens, Georgia, and was printed and bound by Kingsport Press of Kingsport, Tennessee. Book design by Joyce Kachergis Book Design and Production of Bynum, North Carolina.